The Master's Men

The Master's Men

by

John MacArthur, Jr.

WORD OF GRACE COMMUNICATIONS

P.O. Box 4000

Panorama City, CA 91412

Library of Congress Cataloging-in-Publication Data

MacArthur, John F.
  The Master's men.

  1. Apostles—Biography.   2. Bible. N.T.—
Biography.   3. Palestine—Biography.   I. Title.
BS2440.M24   1985   226'.0922 [B]   85-25832
ISBN 0-8024-5106-3 (pbk.)

1 2 3 4 5 6 7 Printing/GB/Year 90 89 88 87 86 85

Printed in the United States of America

Contents

These Bible studies are taken from messages delivered by Pastor-Teacher John MacArthur, Jr., at Grace Community Church in Panorama City, California. These messages have been combined into a 6-tape album entitled "The Master's Men." You may purchase this series either in an attractive vinyl cassette album or as individual cassettes. To purchase these tapes, request the album "The Master's Men" or ask for the tapes by their individual GC numbers. Please consult the current price list; then, send your order, making your check payable to:

WORD OF GRACE COMMUNICATIONS
P.O. Box 4000
Panorama City, CA 91412

Or, call the following toll-free number:
1-800-55-GRACE

1

The Messengers of the King

Outline

Introduction

Lesson
I. The Initiation of the Apostles
   A. The Phrase Defining Their Commissioning
   B. The Phases of Their Calling
      1. Conversion
      2. Ministry
      3. Internship
      4. Final sending
   C. The Process of Their Choosing
      1. Chosen sovereignly
      2. Chosen prayerfully
      3. Chosen to be trained
         a) Their lack of spiritual understanding
            (1) Described
               (*a*) Matthew 15:15-16
               (*b*) Luke 18:31-34
               (*c*) John 13:2-17
               (*d*) Matthew 16:21-23
               (*e*) John 21:1-18
            (2) Dealt with
         b) Their lack of humility
            (1) Described
               (*a*) Mark 9:33-37
               (*b*) Matthew 20:20-28
            (2) Dealt with
         c) Their lack of faith
            (1) Described
            (2) Dealt with
         d) Their lack of commitment
            (1) Described
            (2) Dealt with
         e) Their lack of power

Introduction

As we look at Matthew 10:1-4, I basically want to discuss three elements of the commissioning of the twelve: their initiation, their impact, and their identity. This lesson will cover their initiation and their impact, and the next six lessons will deal specifically with their identity.

Now, as we look at the elements behind our Lord's preparation and calling of the twelve, I want us to see how these elements apply in our own lives. I believe this will give us a tremendous pattern for our own understanding of discipleship—how we are to disciple others as well as how God disciples us. This is our Lord's discipling pattern—how He trained the twelve.

Lesson

I. THE INITIATION OF THE APOSTLES (v. 1a)
"And when he had called unto him his twelve disciples."

A. The Phrase Defining Their Commissioning

The Greek verb *proskaleō (kaleō,* "to call"; *pros,* "toward") is an intense word that means "to call to oneself," and carries the idea of a face-to-face calling so that one can receive a commission from another. Matthew 10:1 is Christ's official commissioning of the twelve. He called them to Himself, face to face, to give them their commands, their commission, their instructions. *Proskaleō* is also used in Acts 13:2 where God called out two of the leaders of the church in Antioch, Paul and Barnabas, in an official commissioning.

Notice in Matthew 10:1 that the twelve are referred to as "twelve disciples," then in verse 2 they are "the twelve apostles." They were the disciples when they were learning and the apostles when they were sent. The term "disciple" (Gk., *mathētēs*) means "learner," whereas the term "apostle" (Gk., *apostolos*) comes from the Greek verb *apostellō,* which means "to be sent." First they were learners, then they were sent. So, verses 1-2 show the transition of the twelve from being learners to being sent. Our Lord is calling these men to work with Him in gathering some of His lost, mauled, exhausted, prostrate, shepherdless sheep. It was time for them to evangelize *"the lost sheep of the house of Israel"* (Matt.

10:6) and to preach that *"the kingdom of heaven is at hand"* (Matt. 10:7). This was a critical point in the training of the twelve.

B. The Phases of Their Calling

1. Conversion

In John 1:35-51 we are given an illustration of the initial calling to conversion, or salvation, that our Lord used in the lives of the twelve. He called many to conversion, but John 1 pinpoints this calling of several of the twelve. In this phase, they went with Him for a while, but then returned to their secular employment and to their homes.

2. Ministry

The second phase in the calling of the twelve is illustrated in Matthew 4:18-22. At this point, I believe that Peter, Andrew, James, and John had already been converted; they had already affirmed that Jesus was the Messiah. But here Jesus calls them to leave their nets (their secular employment) and their homes to follow Him exclusively and totally. This is their calling into ministry.

In phase one of their calling, they were called to salvation, and in phase two, Jesus called them to attach themselves to Him permanently, in order to make them into fishers of men. This second phase could be seen as their education. As grown men, they were called away from their employment and livelihood to follow Jesus and be personally trained by Him. This was their schooling.

3. Internship

The third phase of their calling is recorded in our text of Matthew 10. This is their initial sending out. Mark 6:7 tells us that in this initial sending they were sent out two by two. At this stage they really weren't ready to go out alone, so they went along with someone else for support. In fact, in this phase, the Lord stuck closely with them. He was like a mother eagle, watching His eaglets as they began to fly. They were always checking back with Him, letting Him know how it was going. This was their internship—a time for them to go out on their first short-term mission assignment to get a feel for what it was like out in the field. After a season of their personal labor, they returned to the Lord and remained with Him for an extended period of teaching, which, by the way, was more profitable because they now knew where the trouble was and what the things were they needed to know.

4. Final sending

The fourth phase in the calling of the twelve occurred after Christ's resurrection and ascension. After He went back into heaven, He sent the Holy Spirit who indwelt them and scattered them into the world to disciple the nations.

As we come to Matthew 10, the twelve are in phase three. This is their first experience alone in the field, so the Lord doesn't let them out very far—just far enough to learn where the trouble is going to come from. This is their initiation into ministry.

C. The Process of Their Choosing

1. Chosen sovereignly

Matthew 10:1*a* says, "And when he had called unto him his twelve disciples—" Mark 3:13 adds that He called to Himself those "whom he would." It was His choice, His will, His sovereign purpose. There wasn't an executive search. He didn't ask, "How many of you would like to be apostles? Let Me see a show of hands." The twelve were called by the sovereign will and purpose of God. He knew the men He wanted and they weren't even consulted. Their choosing was foreordained like that of Abraham, Moses, Jeremiah, Isaiah, John the Baptist, and even the apostle Paul, who was called into the ministry against his will (see Acts 9:1-6). In John 15:16*a,* Jesus said to the apostles, "Ye have not chosen me, but I have chosen you, and ordained you, that ye should go and bring forth fruit." God sovereignly chose these men—that has always been His pattern. He chose Israel, He chose the apostles, He chooses His church, and He chooses those who serve Him within His church. We who represent Him are "the called according to his purpose" (Rom. 8:28*b*).

2. Chosen prayerfully

Christ chose "whom he would," but in His submission to the Father, He chose the twelve only after He sought the Father's will. This principle applies to us as well, in terms of discipling. As we select those whom we are going to pour our lives into, it should be only after great prayer so that God can show us who it is that we are to give ourselves to. Luke 6:12-13 records for us Christ's night of prayer: "And it came to pass in those days, that he went out into a mountain to pray, and continued all night in prayer to God. And when it was day, he called unto him his disciples; and of them he chose twelve, whom also he named apostles."

They were chosen sovereignly, and they were chosen after a night of prayer, as the submissive Son, in His humility, sought only the will of the Father. John 17:6 affirms that the twelve were indeed the ones the Father gave to the Son, as Jesus said, "I have manifested thy name unto the men whom thou gavest me out of the world; thine they were, and thou gavest them to me."

So, these very special men were chosen by God and affirmed by the Son after a night of prayer.

3. Chosen to be trained

Third, the twelve were chosen to be trained—this was essential. There always has to be a training time, and for them it was a period of three years, walking with the Lord. They left their nets, their boats, their crops, their businesses, their tax-collecting stands—everything—and they wandered around with Jesus. Jesus knew that before they could be sent out, they had to be trained—and what a training they had as they learned directly from the Lord. Learning doesn't really take place by sitting in a class and listening to someone lecture; learning takes place by watching someone's life and observing his pattern of living as he walks through life. Being discipled toward godliness isn't accomplished in a ten-week class; it is accomplished by spending time with a godly individual—walking with him, feeling his heartbeat, hearing him speak, and seeing him pray.

Frankly, it wasn't an easy job to train the twelve. The best of them, Peter, still didn't have a clue as to what he was doing, even after the resurrection. The twelve were really a defective bunch, and we're going to look at their defects. Why? Because when we see what Jesus had to work with and overcome in their lives, it will give us hope that God can also use us.

Basically, the Lord had to deal with five inadequacies.

a) Their lack of spiritual understanding

(1) Described

The Lord chose twelve men to evangelize the world, but they had a problem—they didn't understand the parables and the precepts that He taught. They were thick, dull, stupid, and blind to spiritual truth. In fact, every time the Lord asked them if they understood something that He was teaching, they would reply, "Yes, Lord," but time revealed that they didn't understand at all. They were so dull, they didn't even know when they didn't understand. Let me show you a few examples of their lack of spiritual understanding.

(a) Matthew 15:15-16—"Then answered Peter and said unto him, Explain unto us this parable. And Jesus said, Are ye also yet without understanding?" Jesus rebuked Peter for his lack of spiritual understanding.

(b) Luke 18:31-34—"Then he took unto him the twelve, and said unto them, Behold, we go up to Jerusalem, and all things that are written by the prophets concerning the Son of man shall be accomplished. For he shall be delivered unto the Gentiles, and shall be mocked, and spitefully treated, and spit on; and they shall scourge him, and put him to death. And the third day he shall rise again. And they understood none of these things; and this saying was hidden from them, neither knew they the things which were spoken." They didn't grasp His parables or His precepts, and they didn't understand the prophecies of His suffering. All the while they were saying, "Yes, Lord; we understand"—but they didn't. Don't be fooled by those who think or say they understand—be sure they do.

(c) John 13:2-17—In John 13, Jesus humbled Himself and washed the disciples' feet. But when He came to Peter, note the dialogue between them that reveals Peter's spiritual ignorance: "Then cometh he to Simon Peter; and Peter saith unto him, Lord, dost thou wash my feet? Jesus answered, and said unto him, What I do thou knowest not now, but thou shalt know hereafter. Peter saith unto him, Thou shalt never wash my feet. Jesus answered him, If I wash thee not, thou hast no part with me" (vv. 6-8).

(d) Matthew 16:21-23—Peter's lack of spiritual understanding was never more evident than when he began to rebuke Christ for talking about His future suffering and death. In verse 23 Jesus turned to Peter and said, "Get thee behind me, Satan. Thou art an offense unto me; for thou savorest not the things that are of God, but those that are of men."

12

(*e*) John 21:1-18—It is clear from John 21 that Peter, and six of the other apostles, didn't understand their roles, even after Christ's resurrection. They had gone back to their former occupation of fishing when Jesus came to them in His resurrected form and basically said, "What's going on? Do you love Me, Peter? Then feed My sheep. That's what I called you to do!"

The twelve didn't understand Christ's parables, His precepts, the purpose of His sufferings, or their own roles. They lacked spiritual understanding, which Jesus had to overcome.

(2) Dealt with

How did Jesus deal with the apostles' lack of spiritual understanding? Simply by constantly teaching them. In fact, Acts 1:2-3 tells us that for forty days after His resurrection, Jesus taught the apostles "of the things pertaining to the kingdom of God." He was always dealing with their lack of understanding by instruction.

b) Their lack of humility

(1) Described

The twelve were a proud, jealous, envious bunch. You say, "How can you say that about the apostles?" Well, let me show you.

(*a*) Mark 9:33-37—"And they came to Capernaum; and, being in the house, he asked them, What was it that ye disputed among yourselves on the way?" You see, all the while they were walking to Capernaum, the apostles were fighting about something; so Jesus asked them what it was all about. Verse 34 says, "But they held their peace; for on the way they had disputed among themselves, who should be the greatest." All the time our dear Lord was walking along, these twelve selfless, humble souls were fighting about who was going to be the greatest. Well, in verses 35-37, the Lord proceeds to sit them down and give them a lesson on humility.

(*b*) Matthew 20:20-28—The argument about who would be the greatest in the kingdom got so hot that James and John had the gall to get their mother involved in the dispute. In Matthew 20:20 we read, "Then came to him the mother of Zebedee's children with her sons, worshiping him, and desiring a certain thing of him. And he said unto her, What wilt thou? She said unto him, Grant that these, my two sons, may sit, the one on thy right hand, and the other on the left, in thy kingdom." Now that was really brash. James and John wanted it badly, yet they didn't even have the courage to ask Jesus personally—they got their mother to do it. Can you picture them standing there beside their mother while she asked Jesus for such a ridiculously selfish thing?

Verse 22 continues, "But Jesus answered and said, Ye know not what ye ask. Are ye able to drink of the cup that I shall drink of, and to be baptized with the baptism that I am baptized with? They say unto him, We are able. And he saith unto them, Ye shall drink indeed of my cup, and be baptized with the baptism that I am baptized with." Jesus was referring here to the martyrdom of James and the persecution and exile of John. He told them that they were going to go through the pain, the suffering, and the anguish, but then He said, "But to sit on my right hand, and on my left, is not mine to give, but it shall be given to them for whom it is prepared by my Father."

Look at the reaction of the other apostles when they heard what James and John were trying to do: "And when the ten heard it, they were moved with indignation against the two brethren" (v. 24). Why were they furious? Was it because they wouldn't stand for such pride? No. It was because James and John went in front of the others to try and get those places of honor. The apostles' indignation wasn't righteous; it was selfish.

In verses 27-28, Jesus said to them, "And whosoever will be chief among you, let him be your servant; even as the Son of man came not to be ministered unto, but to minister, and to give his life a ransom for many."

(2) Dealt with

How did Jesus deal with their lack of humility? I believe He dealt with it by giving them a demonstration of His own humility. He likened Himself to a little child in Mark 9:37; He likened Himself to a servant in

Matthew 20:28; and He washed the disciples' feet in John 13, followed by the statement, "A new commandment I give unto you, that ye love one another; as I have loved you, that ye also love one another" (v. 34).

He overcame their lack of spiritual understanding by instruction and their lack of humility by example—the example of His own life.

c) Their lack of faith

(1) Described

The apostles had a third problem—they had a lack of faith. They didn't believe God. In fact, probably the most common phrase Jesus said to them was "O ye of little faith" (Matt. 6:30; 8:26; 14:31; 16:8). In Mark 4:40 He said to them, "How is it that ye have no faith?" Mark 16:14, at the end of Mark's gospel, says that Jesus rebuked the apostles because of "their unbelief and hardness of heart, because they believed not those who had seen him after he had risen." They didn't even believe the reports of the resurrection. What a bunch to work with! And just think, Jesus was supposed to transform these men into men who were going to change the world.

(2) Dealt with

How did Jesus deal with their lack of faith and unbelief? By performing miracles and mighty deeds, and by repeatedly showing them His power. In fact, I believe that Jesus did the miracles primarily for the disciples, not for the crowds. After the crucifixion, the disciples needed to be absolutely sure and confident in His resurrection, so He appeared to them, let them touch Him and see Him, and "showed himself alive after his passion by many infallible proofs" (Acts 1:3*a*).

So Jesus overcame their lack of understanding with teaching, their lack of humility with example, and their lack of faith with miracles and mighty deeds. All of this was part of the teaching process.

d) Their lack of commitment

(1) Described

The apostles had a fourth problem—a lack of commitment. They would say, "Oh, we will never forsake You or deny You"—but when it came down to the crisis hour that Christ needed them most, they were gone. Judas betrayed Him, Peter denied Him, and the other ten just took off—they couldn't handle it. It's interesting that Luke 5:11 says that when Jesus called His disciples "they forsook all, and followed him," but Mark 14:50 says, "They all forsook him, and fled." They deserted Christ when they saw the swords, the staves, the lanterns, and the Romans. When they started to smell death, they got out.

(2) Dealt with

How did Jesus deal with their lack of commitment? In Luke 22:31-32a we see how Jesus dealt with Peter's lack of commitment: "And the Lord said, Simon, Simon, behold, Satan hath desired to have you, that he may sift you as wheat; but I have prayed for thee, that thy faith fail not." *Jesus dealt with their lack of commitment through prayer.*

In John 15:18-21 and 16:1-3, Jesus tells His disciples that they're going to be persecuted, hated, despised, and even killed. But then immediately in chapter 17, He begins to pray for them, and in verse 15 He says, "I pray not that thou shouldest take them out of the world, but that thou shouldest keep them from the evil." Jesus prayed for their lack of commitment.

e) Their lack of power

(1) Described

The apostles had a fifth problem—a lack of power. They were weak and helpless. This is illustrated in Matthew 17:14-21: "And when they were come to the multitude, there came to him a certain man, kneeling down to him, and saying, Lord, have mercy on my son; for he is epileptic, and greatly vexed; for often he falleth into the fire, and often into the water. And I brought him to thy disciples, and they could not cure him. Then Jesus answered and said, O faithless and perverse generation, how long shall I be with you? How long shall I bear with you? Bring him here to me. And Jesus rebuked the demon, and he departed out of him; and the child was cured from that very hour. Then came the disciples to Jesus privately, and said, Why could not we cast him out? And Jesus said unto them, Because of your unbelief; for verily I say unto you, If ye have faith as a grain of mustard seed, ye shall say unto this mountain, Move from here to yonder place; and it shall move; and nothing shall be impossible unto you. Howbeit, this kind goeth not out except by prayer and fasting."

(2) Dealt with

How did Jesus deal with their lack of power? I believe He dealt with this problem in a marvelous way. John 20:22 says, "He breathed on them, and saith unto them, Receive ye the Holy Spirit." And Acts 1:8*a* says, "But ye shall receive power, after the Holy Spirit is come upon you."

The twelve were chosen sovereignly by God to be the associates of Christ to found the church. They were chosen through prayer, and they were chosen to be trained. In their training, Christ had to overcome their lack of spiritual understanding through instruction, their lack of humility through example, their lack of faith through wonderous miracles, their lack of commitment through prayer, and their lack of power through the agency of the Spirit of God in their lives.

Well, He accomplished His task—they were transformed. Acts 4:13 says that when the Sanhedrin "saw the boldness of Peter and John, and perceived that they were unlearned and ignorant men, they marveled; and they took knowledge of them, that they had been with Jesus." How did they know that they had been with Jesus? I'll tell you how they knew—they *did* the same things Jesus did, they *said* the same things Jesus said, and they *loved* the same way Jesus loved. *When Jesus finished with them, they went out as living mirrors, reflecting Him.* In fact that's why people finally wound up calling them Christians (i.e., "little Christs").

Luke 6:40 says it all. Jesus said, "A pupil is not above his teacher; but everyone, after he has been fully trained, will be like his teacher" (NASB*). Jesus trained them in three years, and when they went out, they were like their teacher. Graduation day is in John 15:15*a* when Jesus says, "Henceforth I call you not servants . . . but I have called you friends."

Just think of what they learned by being with Christ for those three years. He transformed their lives, and as a result they transformed the world. Imagine walking with Jesus every day,

New American Standard Bible.

17

continuously hearing His matchless wisdom. Imagine being with someone who never lost His temper, but was only righteously indignant over things that took glory from God; who cared absolutely nothing for Himself, but instead gave Himself to everybody else; who was totally consumed with helping others, continuously to the point of fatigue; who loved everyone, raised the dead, healed the sick, and gave sight to the blind and hearing to the deaf. Well, it certainly had an effect on the twelve. They were with Him and they became like Him. That's how the process of discipleship works.

So they were chosen sovereignly, they were chosen after a night of prayer, they were chosen to be trained, and finally, they were:

4. Chosen to be sent

Matthew 10:1 says, "And when he had called unto him his twelve disciples." Then verse 2 says, "Now the names of the twelve apostles are these." A transition is made here from "disciple" (Gk., *mathētēs*, "learner") to "apostle" (Gk., *apostolos*, "sent one"). The word *apostle* is derived from the Greek verb *apostellō*. *Stellō* means "to dispatch," and *apo* means "away from." *Apostellō,* then, means "to dispatch away from." In classical Greek, the word is used almost exclusively to speak of a naval expedition dispatched to serve a foreign city or a foreign country. In a similar way, the disciples became "sent ones," or apostles.

It's not enough to be saved or to be called to serve Christ or to be trained. When all of that is done, we must go out into all the world and make disciples (Matt. 28:19-20). We have been made disciples in order to make disciples. We are to carry on the same discipling process that our Lord used with the twelve. Are you being discipled—learning with a view to being sent out? Are you discipling—training someone with a view to sending him to reach others? Discipleship and apostleship go together. First, an individual is to follow, then he is to leave and carry the message.

As we come to Matthew 10, the twelve are being sent out on their first short-term mission assignment. This is where they will learn by doing. During this internship phase, they will run into all kinds of problems. But when they return, Jesus will use those experiences to teach them. In the fourth and final phase of their calling, the Holy Spirit will fill them, and they will go out, baptizing and teaching all nations. This is the marvelous pattern of their initiation.

II. THE IMPACT OF THE APOSTLES (v. 1*b*)

"He gave them the power against unclean spirits, to cast them out, and to heal all manner of sickness and all manner of disease."

Why did Jesus give the apostles this power? To demonstrate that they were from Christ. They were able to do the very same things that Christ did. If you follow their miracles through the book of Acts you will see that they cast out demons, healed the sick, and basically manifested the same kingdom power that Jesus manifested. And because they were inseparably linked with Christ they had a tremendous impact—they turned Jerusalem upside down, and then they turned the world upside down. Everywhere they went, people were converted because of their impact.

In verse 2, Matthew talks about the identity of the apostles—but we'll look at that in our next lesson.

Focusing on the Facts

1. What is the importance of Matthew 10:1 for the twelve disciples (see p. 8)?
2. What does *disciple* mean? What does *apostle* mean? Describe the transition that occurs in Matthew 10:1-2 (see p. 8).
3. Describe the four phases of Christ's calling of the twelve disciples (see pp. 9-10).
4. Who was responsible for choosing who the twelve disciples would be (see pp. 10-11)?
5. What did Jesus do before He chose the twelve (Luke 6:12-13; see p. 10)?
6. How does someone learn best? How did the disciples receive their training (see p. 11)?
7. Why didn't the disciples understand the parables and precepts that the Lord taught? Give some examples (see pp. 11-12).
8. How did Jesus deal with the disciples' lack of understanding (see p. 12)?
9. What did James and John have their mother ask Jesus? What was the reaction of the other ten disciples (Matt. 20:20-24; see pp. 13-14)?
10. How did Jesus deal with the disciples' lack of humility (see pp. 14-15)?
11. What are some of the things that reveal the disciples' lack of faith? How did Jesus deal with that (see p. 15)?
12. What did the disciples do at the hour that Jesus needed them most (see pp. 15-16)?
13. How did Jesus deal with the disciples' lack of commitment (see p. 16)?

14. According to Matthew 17:20, why couldn't the disciples cast a demon out of a certain man's son (see pp. 16-17)?
15. How did Jesus deal with the disciples' lack of power (see p. 17)?
16. According to Acts 4:13, the Sanhedrin realized that the disciples had been with Jesus. How did they know that (see p. 17)?
17. What did the disciples become, according to Matthew 10:2? What were they sent to do (see p. 18)?
18. What was the purpose of the assignment that Jesus gave the disciples in Matthew 10:1 (see p. 18)?
19. What kind of power did Jesus give His disciples in Matthew 10:1? Why (see p. 19)?

Pondering the Principles

1. Look up the following verses: John 15:16; Romans 8:28; Ephesians 1:4; 2:10; 2 Thessalonians 2:13. What do those verses indicate about your salvation? According to Ephesians 2:10, why were you saved? Thank God for your salvation right now. To see all that your salvation means to you, meditate on Ephesians 1:3-23. Thank God for all that He has given you.
2. To train the disciples, Jesus spent the last three years of His life with them. When His Holy Spirit came upon them after His ascension, they reflected Christ to the world. You can do the same thing, but you need to spend time with Christ to do it. Make up a schedule (one that you can keep up with) for reading through the gospels. You may want to obtain a harmony of the gospels to help in your study. Commit yourself to daily communion with the Lord as you learn about Him through His words and His works.
3. Do you have a problem with pride? Don't feel bad; we all do. But of all sins, pride can be the most destructive. Look up the following verses: Proverbs 8:13; 16:18; 1 Corinthians 8:1-2; Galatians 6:3. What does God have to say about pride? How can you have victory over your prideful heart? Look up the following verses: Proverbs 11:2; 16:19; Philippians 2:3; James 4:6. What is God's answer to a prideful heart? Make the commitment to what God wants from you. When you see that you are being prideful in an area of your life, confess it right away. Ask God to replace it with a humble spirit.
4. Read Matthew 28:19-20. How are you responding to Christ's Great Commission? All Christians have received that calling. Where are you in the discipling process? Have you been discipled? Has someone taught you for the purpose of going out to reach others for Christ? If you are past that stage, are you a discipler? Are you presently training someone so that you can eventually send him out to reach others for Christ? You should be in one of those stages. If you aren't, then get busy. Begin to fulfill God's calling in your life.

2

Peter: A Lesson in Leadership

Outline

Introduction

Review
I. The Initiation of the Apostles
II. The Impact of the Apostles

Lesson
III. The Identity of the Apostles (Matt. 10:2-4)
    1. Peter is always mentioned first, and Judas always last
    2. Each list has three groups containing the same four members
       a) Group one
       b) Group two
       c) Group three
    3. Each group contains a decreasing amount of information about its members
    4. The groups are in a decreasing order of intimacy to Christ
    5. In every list, each of the three groups starts with the same name
    6. Among the apostles there were extreme contrasts in temperament
       a) Peter and John
          (1) Peter
          (2) John
       b) Nathanael and Thomas
          (1) Nathanael
          (2) Thomas
       c) Matthew and Simon the Zealot
          (1) Matthew
          (2) Simon the Zealot
  A. Simon Peter
    1. The right raw material
       a) Inquisitiveness
       b) Initiative
       c) Involvement

2. The right experiences
    a) His great revelation
    b) His great reward
    c) His great remission
    d) His great rejection
    e) His great recommissioning
    f) His great realization
3. The right lessons
    a) Submission
    b) Restraint
    c) Humility
    d) Sacrifice
    e) Love
    f) Courage

Introduction

The twelve men introduced to us in the first part of Matthew 10 are the foundation of the church. In Ephesians 2:20, it says that the household of God is "built upon the foundation of the apostles and prophets, Jesus Christ himself being the chief corner stone." Matthew 10:1 calls these twelve men "disciples" (lit., "learners"), but in verse 2 a transition is made and they are referred to as "apostles" (lit., "sent ones"). They started out as learners and became sent ones.

Now, these apostles were not only the ones who were foundational in terms of leadership and authority, but they were the ones who received divine revelation (Eph. 3:5), were responsible for writing most of the New Testament, and were the framers of the theology of the early church (Acts 2:42—"the apostles' doctrine"). According to Ephesians 4:12, the apostles were given to the church "for the perfecting of the saints for the work of the ministry for the edifying of the body of Christ." And in addition to the important words they gave, their lives were examples of virtue. This is why, I believe, they are referred to as the "holy apostles" (Eph. 3:5; Rev. 18:20). They set the pattern for a godly, holy, virtuous life.

So, they were the foundation. And as such, it's essential for us to see how the Lord worked with them, how He discipled them, how He trained them, and how He sent them, thus giving us a pattern for discipling others and sending them to reach the world.

Review

I. THE INITIATION OF THE APOSTLES (Matt. 10:1*a*)

In our last study, we saw four phases in the calling of the twelve. First, He called them to Himself by way of conversion. Second, He called them away from their normal life-style into full-time training. Third, He sent them out as interns—to get their feet wet. That is what is about to take place in Matthew 10. They had been instructed, possibly for as long as eighteen months, and they still had many more months of instruction ahead of them, but in this internship phase, He sent them out on their own, two by two, to gain some experience, to hit the wall a few times, and to fail as well as succeed. So, the disciples were sent out, and when they came back, the Lord was able to interact with them and teach them even more effectively. The fourth and final phase occurred when the Spirit of God filled them and they were sent into the whole world to disciple the nations (Acts 1).

Here in Matthew 10, the twelve are beginning phase three. This is their first opportunity to go out on their own, two by two. The Lord, however, will stay close enough to them to watch them, to see how they fare, and to teach them from the experiences that they're about to have.

II. THE IMPACT OF THE APOSTLES (Matt. 10:1*b*)

In our last lesson we also looked briefly at the power, or authority, that the Lord gave to the twelve. We saw that they were basically able to do two things with this divine authority—cast out the vile, evil, wretched, unclean demons, and heal all manner of disease and sickness. Now, the reason Christ gave them power over demons (the gift of miracles) and power over disease (the gift of healing) was to confirm their message. Matthew 10:6-7 tells us that the primary task in their internship phase was to preach. It says, "But go, rather, to the lost sheep of the house of Israel. And as ye go, preach, saying, The kingdom of heaven is at hand." But on what basis would the people hear their message? Their impact came when they performed the marvelous works of casting out demons (showing they had power over the kingdom of darkness) and healing (showing they had power over disease). So as they went out preaching, they were also healing and casting out demons as an affirmation that they were indeed representatives of God (cf. Heb. 2:3-4).

Lesson

III. THE IDENTITY OF THE APOSTLES (Matt. 10:2-4)

"Now the names of the twelve apostles are these: the first, Simon, who is called Peter, and Andrew, his brother; James, the son of Zebedee, and John, his brother; Philip and Bartholomew; Thomas and Matthew, the tax collector; James, the son of Alphaeus, and Lebbaeus, whose surname was Thaddaeus; Simon, the Canaanite, and Judas Iscariot, who also betrayed him."

Frankly, these were just ordinary men. The only one who may have had some special wealth was Matthew—but he gained it through extortion. None of them had any particular academic background. As far as we know, none of them had any social status. They were just common people—some of them still utterly unknown to us. But the twelve were chosen from the common people to be the agents of Christ and to set in motion the advancement of the kingdom. *Throughout the history of the world there has never been a task equal to the task given these men—to finish the work that Jesus began.*

Now, before we begin to look specifically at each of the apostles, I want to make some observations of the list itself.

There are four lists of the apostles—Matthew 10, Mark 3, Luke 6, and Acts 1—and all four lists contain some marvelous similarities. For example:

1. Peter is always mentioned first, and Judas always last.

   Why is Peter mentioned first? Was he the first one chosen? No, he wasn't the first one chosen, but he was first (Gk., *prōtos*) in the sense of rank. Peter was the foremost, not in terms of authority or essence, but in terms of function. In other words, Peter was the leader of the twelve, and each of the four lists points this out.

2. Each list has three groups containing the same four members.

   a) Group one: Peter, Andrew, James, John

   b) Group two: Philip, Bartholomew (or Nathanael), Thomas, Matthew

   c) Group three: James the son of Alphaeus, Lebbaeus (or Thaddaeus), Simon the Zealot, Judas Iscariot

   Each group always has the same four people in it. Their names may be in a different order within the group, but they always stay in the same group.

3. Each group contains a decreasing amount of information about its members.

   In other words, we know a lot about those in group one: Peter, Andrew, James, and John; a little less about those in group two: Philip, Nathanael, Thomas, and Matthew; and very little about those in group three, except for Judas—and what we know about him, we wouldn't care to know. So, there's a decreasing amount of information about each group.

4. The groups are in a decreasing order of intimacy to Christ.

The Lord was very, very close to those in group one, somewhat close to those in group two, and we don't know that He was close at all to those in group three. This points out a very important factor in leadership—a leader can't be intimate with everybody. It's impossible. In fact, out of the four in group one, our Lord drew closer to three of them. And out of those three, He spent most of His time with Peter. Frankly, He had to spend most of His time with Peter because He couldn't get Peter off His back. Peter trailed Christ everywhere, constantly asking Him questions. So the Lord was closest to those in group one, but the function and ministry of those in group two and three were just as important. However, it's interesting that those apostles who wrote portions of the New Testament came mostly from group one.

5. In every list, each of the three groups starts with the same name.

In the different lists, each of the three groups contains the same names, but not necessarily in the same order within the group. However, the first name in each group is always the same: Peter, in group one; Philip, in group two; and James, the son of Alphaeus, in group three. Do you know what this tells us? Each individual group had a leader. Peter was the leader of the twelve and of group one, but there was also a leader of each of the other two groups.

6. Among the apostles there were extreme contrasts in temperament.

   a) Peter and John

      (1) Peter—Peter was a man of action, impulsive and eager. I call him the apostle with the foot-shaped mouth because he was always sticking his foot in it. He was always blurting out, charging ahead in a mad hurry.

      (2) John—In the same group with Peter was a man by the name of John. He was a quiet, contemplative man of prayer, a loving heart who reclined on the breast of Jesus.

   It must have been interesting for Peter and John to work together, as they did in the first twelve chapters of Acts. I'm sure Peter was wanting to charge all the time, saying, "John, will you get up? Let's get going!" while John probably replied, "Just wait, Peter, I'm meditating." You can imagine how frustrating it was for both of them, but God taught them marvelous lessons.

    b) Nathanael and Thomas

        (1) Nathanael—Nathanael is seen as always ready to believe. In John 1, he just accepted the facts. He didn't seem to doubt anything, he was willing to receive it all.

        (2) Thomas—Thomas was quite a contrast to Nathanael. He was skeptical and wouldn't believe anything unless he could see it and touch it.

    c) Matthew and Simon the Zealot

        (1) Matthew—Matthew worked for the Roman government extorting taxes.

        (2) Simon the Zealot—A Zealot was a radical revolutionary whose goal was to overthrow Rome. Frankly, if Simon had met Matthew anywhere but in the presence of Jesus, he would have stuck a dagger in him!

So, within the twelve there were political differences, spiritual differences, and basic emotional differences—and the Lord was to take this conglomeration of people and change the world. The wonderful story is that they *did* change the world—they didn't fail.

Now, let's look at the first apostle in the list given in Matthew 10:2-4.

A. Simon Peter

As we look at Simon Peter, I want us to focus on the question *How does God build a leader?* Peter is the key to understanding the answer to this question. The gospels are literally filled with his name. In fact, Peter's name is mentioned in the gospels more than any name but Jesus'. Nobody speaks as often as Peter, and nobody is spoken to by the Lord as often as Peter. No disciple is so reproved by the Lord as Peter, and no disciple reproves the Lord but Peter. No disciple ever so boldly confessed and outspokenly acknowledged the lordship of Christ as Peter, and no one denied it as boldly as Peter. No one is so praised and so blessed as Peter, and no one else is called Satan but Peter. The Lord had harder things to say to Peter than He ever said to anybody else—but that was part of making him the man He wanted him to be.

Now how does God take such an ambivalent character, such a contradiction in human flesh, and make him a leader? I think there are basically three elements.

1. The right raw material

The Lord recognized in Peter the right raw material for leadership. I'm convinced that Peter was the leader before anybody even acknowledged it. He probably just took over—that's the way he was. He had the raw material for leadership. What is the raw material looked for in a leader?

a) Inquisitiveness

The first thing to look for in a leader is whether or not he asks questions. People who don't ask questions don't wind up as leaders because they're not concerned about problems and solutions. If you want to find a leader, look for someone who asks questions.

In the gospel records, Peter asks more questions than all the other apostles combined. For example, it was Peter who asked the meaning of a difficult saying (Matt. 15:15; Luke 12:41). It was Peter who asked how often he had to forgive (Matt. 18:21). It was Peter who asked about the reward of those who had left all to follow Jesus (Matt. 19:27). It was Peter who asked about the fig tree that had withered away (Mark 11:21). It was Peter who asked the meaning of things that Jesus had said about the approaching end (Mark 13:3). And it was Peter who asked questions of the risen Christ (John 21:20-22). Peter was always asking questions—but that's the raw material of leadership.

b) Initiative

The second element of leadership is initiative. Peter not only asked all the questions, but he was always the one to answer any questions posed by Christ. For example, it was Peter who answered when Jesus asked who had touched Him in the crowd (Luke 8:45), and it was Peter who answered Jesus' question to the disciples, "But who say ye that I am?" (Matt. 16:15-16). Peter was always replying, always taking the initiative.

c) Involvement

A third element of the raw material of leadership is involvement. Leaders are always right in the middle of the action. They go through life with a cloud of dust around them. For example, who, out of all the disciples, jumped out of a boat and walked on water? Peter (Matt. 14:29). Now people always look at this incident and criticize Peter's lack of faith. Well, Peter *did* sink because of his lack of faith, *but the rest of the disciples never even got out of the boat!* Before you criticize Peter, remember where he was when he began to sink! People look at Peter's life and say, "Peter denied the Lord." That's true, but he was confronted with that because he had enough courage to follow Jesus all the way to the house of the high priest—other disciples had fled. Peter was always in the middle of the action. When the resurrection came, who were the first disciples at the tomb? Peter and John. When John arrived, slightly before Peter, he stooped down and looked in, but Peter just rushed right in. He was always in the middle of everything.

So I think the Lord saw in Peter the right raw material for leadership: inquisitiveness, initiative, and involvement.

Why did Jesus change Simon's name to Peter?

Simon was a very, very common name. When Simon met Jesus he was a fisherman by trade and lived with his brother Andrew, also a fisherman. Originally, he was from the village of Bethsaida, but he later moved to Capernaum. We know that Simon was married because the Lord healed his mother-in-law (Luke 4:38) and because Paul made mention of the fact that Cephas (Peter) took his wife along on his apostolic mission (1 Cor. 9:5). So the fisherman named Simon had a common name, a common trade, and a common marital status, but the Lord saw the raw material for leadership.

By nature, Simon tended to shift and vacillate, so the Lord changed his name to try to force into his subliminal thinking what He wanted him to be. He changed his name from Simon to Peter (Greek), or Cephas (Aramaic), which means "stone." At first, it must have been a contradiction calling "shifting" Simon "Stone," but I'm sure that every time Jesus called him by that name, he thought, *I must be solid and firm. I must be a stone.* I believe the Lord gave him this name to force his thinking down that path.

Now every time the Lord spoke to Peter, He could designate what He wanted to say to him by the name He used. If He called him Peter (Stone), he got one message; if He called him Simon, he got another message; and if He called him Simon Peter, still another message.

Even after his name was changed, *the name Simon was always*

28

used in two cases. First of all, it was used to designate him in a *secular* way. For example: "the house of Simon" (Mark 1:29); "Simon's wife's mother" (Mark 1:30; Luke 4:38); Simon's boat (Luke 5:3); Simon's fishing partners (Luke 5:10); "Simon's house" (Luke 4:38; Acts 10:17). In other words, his secular identification was Simon.

Second, the name Simon was used when he was being *reprimanded for sin.* When the Lord wanted to focus on his sinfulness, He called him Simon. For example, in Luke 5:4 the Lord tells Simon, "Launch out into the deep, and let down your nets for a draught." Well, they had been fishing all night and had not caught anything, and I can just hear Peter mumbling, "Oh, man, that's ridiculous. Does He think we don't know what we're doing? We fish for a profession and He's telling us how to fish?" Verses 6-7 tell us that when Simon let down his nets, there were so many fish that the nets broke and the boats began to sink. It's evident that the Lord unmasked Simon's sin when he said to the Lord, "Depart from me; for I am a sinful man, O Lord" (v. 8*b*).

Another example of Simon in his sinfulness is seen in John 21. Acting in disobedience, he went back to his profession of fishing after Christ had specifically called him to preach. In verses 15-17, the resurrected Jesus confronts him on the shore and asks him three times, "Simon, son of Jonah, lovest thou me?"

So, Peter is seen as Simon in his *sinful* and *secular* identification and as Peter in his *spiritual* identification. Remember, the Lord was going to make him into a stone—firm and solid.

It's interesting to note that in the gospel of John, Peter is called Simon Peter seventeen times. I think this is because John knew him so well. He knew him as always being in a flux somewhere between Simon and Peter. In fact, the whole life of Peter can be outlined by his names: Simon, Simon Peter, Peter—thus showing his transition. I think that John knew him so well, he just called him Simon Peter because he could never figure out when he was being Simon and when Peter.

How did the Lord take a guy with this kind of raw material and make him into a leader? First of all, He recognized his raw material. Second, He brought into his life:

2. The right experiences

We learn most effectively from our experiences, so the Lord allowed Peter to have some life-changing ones.

a) His great revelation

In John chapter 6, Jesus has given a tremendous message presenting Himself as the Bread of Life, and some people cannot understand it all. So, according to verse 66, "From that time many of his disciples went back, and walked no more with him." Then verse 67 continues, "Then said Jesus unto the twelve, Will ye also go away? Then Simon Peter answered him, Lord, to whom shall we go? Thou hast the words of eternal life. And we believe and are sure that thou art that Christ, the Son of the living God." I think after Peter said that he must have grabbed his mouth and said, "Where did that come from?" That was a startling statement. In fact, I believe it was a revelation from God. I believe he started to open his mouth and God talked right through him.

Peter had the same kind of revelatory experience again in Matthew 16:15-16. Jesus asks the disciples in verse 15, "But who say ye that I am?" And immediately in verse 16 Peter answers, "Thou art the Christ, the Son of the living God." What a tremendous statement! In fact, Jesus confirms that Peter's statement was a revelation from God in verse 17: "And Jesus answered and said unto him. Blessed art thou, Simon Barjona; for flesh and blood hath not revealed it unto thee, but my Father, who is in heaven."

Jesus was transforming Peter by letting him know that God wanted to use his mouth—that God could speak through him. God gave him the experience of revelation because one day he was going to stand up on the day of Pentecost and *preach* the revelation of God. And one day he was going to take a pen and *write* the revelation of God. Jesus prepared him with a revelatory experience, giving him the sense that God was moving and was there.

b) His great reward

Second, the Lord gives Peter a tremendous reward, or promise, in Matthew 16:18-19. After Peter's confession of Christ in verse 16, Jesus says, "I say also unto thee, That thou art Peter (Gk., *petros*, 'stone'), and upon this rock (Gk., *petra*, 'bedrock' or 'massive stone'; i.e., the rock of his confession) I will build my church, and the gates of hades shall not prevail against it. And I will give unto thee the keys of the kingdom of heaven." You say, "In what way did Peter unlock the kingdom of heaven?" Well, who preached the first great apostolic sermon? Peter did, on the day of Pentecost (Acts 2:14-40). To whom did he preach it? The Jews. Which apostle led the first Gentile to Christ? Peter led Cornelius to Christ (Acts 10). Peter unlocked the door to the kingdom of heaven to the Jews and to the Gentiles.

c) His great remission

In Matthew 16:21 Peter is really feeling his oats. In verse 16 he is given a revelation, and in verse 19 he is given the keys of the kingdom of heaven. He is really feeling like a leader. Verse 21 says, "From that time forth began Jesus to show unto his disciples, how he must go unto Jerusalem, and suffer many things from the elders and chief priests and scribes, and be killed, and be raised again the third day." Jesus tells His disciples that He's going to suffer and die—but look at Peter's reaction in verse 22: "Then Peter took him, and began to rebuke him." Peter took the Lord, the Creator of the universe, and said, "Come with me. I've got to straighten You out." Peter was unbelievable! He got a little taste of power and he really started feeling his oats. The danger was, he didn't know what his limits were.

Well, he took the Lord and began rebuking Him, saying, "Be it far from thee, Lord; this shall not be unto thee." In other words, "As long as I'm in charge, nothing's going to happen to You. I'll promise You that." The Lord's reply to Peter is in verse 23: "But he turned and said unto Peter, Get thee behind me, Satan. Thou art an offense unto me; for thou savorest not the things that are of God, but those that are of men." In other words, "Peter, you don't know the plan of God; you're only thinking from the human viewpoint." In verse 16 Peter's mouth had been used for God, but here in verse 22 it is used for Satan. He was doing exactly what Satan had done during Christ's temptation—trying to derail Him from going to the cross. *Peter was just as available to the devil as he was to God,* and that is a great lesson for a leader to learn. The greater potential a person has to be used by God, the greater potential he has to be used by Satan.

d) His great rejection

In Matthew 26:31 the Lord gives a prophecy regarding the shepherd being smitten and the sheep scattered. This referred to His disciples leaving Him and running away. However, in verse 33, Peter speaks up and says, "Though all men shall be offended because of thee, yet will I never be offended." In other words, "I'm not like all men. I'm a cut above the rest. They may all forsake You but I'll never do that." Verses 34 and 35 continue, "Jesus said unto him, Verily I say unto thee that this night, before the cock crows, thou shalt deny me thrice. Peter said unto him, Though I should die with thee, yet will I not deny thee. Likewise also said all the disciples."

Well, Peter had great confidence—but he rejected and denied Jesus. Look at verses 69-75 of chapter 26: "Now Peter sat outside in the court, and a maid came unto him, saying, Thou also wast with Jesus of Galilee. But he denied it before them all, saying, I know not what thou sayest. And when he was gone out into the porch, another maid saw him, and said unto them that were there, This fellow was also with Jesus of Nazareth. And again he denied with an oath, I do not know the man. And after a while came unto him they that stood by, and said to Peter, Surely thou also art one of them; for thy speech betrayeth thee. Then began he to curse and to swear, saying, I know not the man. And immediately the cock crowed. And Peter remembered the word of Jesus, who said unto him, Before the cock crows, thou shalt deny me thrice. And he went out, and wept bitterly." That was quite a lesson!

e) His great recommissioning

In John 21, Peter goes fishing in disobedience to the Lord's call for him to preach, but the Lord doesn't let him catch any fish. When Peter comes to shore, Jesus gives him an experience he will never forget—He confronts his lack of love: "So when they had dined, Jesus saith to Simon Peter, Simon, son of Jonah, lovest thou me more than these? He saith unto him, Yea, Lord; thou knowest that I love thee. He saith unto him, Feed my lambs. He saith to him again the second time, Simon, son of Jonah, lovest thou me? He saith unto him, Yea, Lord; thou knowest that I love thee. He saith unto him, Feed my sheep. He saith unto him the third time, Simon, son of Jonah, lovest thou me? And he said unto him, Lord, thou knowest all things; thou knowest that I love thee. Jesus saith unto him, Feed my sheep" (vv. 15-17). Then at the end of verse 19 Jesus says to Peter, "Follow me." That was Peter's recommissioning.

Peter's great revelation, reward, remission, rejection, and recommissioning were all key experiences in his life—and they all led up to

f) His great realization

Peter finally became the man God wanted him to be, and his experiences were part of making him into that man.

3. The right lessons

What are the lessons a leader needs to learn? Let's look at Peter and use him as our pattern.

a) Submission

Leaders tend to be confident, outgoing, overt, eager, and aggressive. Therefore, the first lesson a leader needs to learn is submission.

In Matthew 17:24-27 the Lord tells Peter to go fishing and that the first fish he caught would contain a coin in its mouth with which they would pay their taxes. Now, knowing Peter, you might assume that he wouldn't pay any attention to taxation. He would probably say, "Hey, we're in this kingdom business. I don't have time to mess with taxes and to fool with this passing world."

But Jesus taught Peter to be submissive to the powers that are ordained of God.

Peter learned his lesson. In 1 Peter 2:13-18 he writes, "Submit yourselves to every ordinance of man for the Lord's sake, whether it be to the king, as supreme, or unto governors, as unto them that are sent by him for the punishment of evildoers, and for the praise of them that do well. For so is the will of God, that with well-doing ye may put to silence the ignorance of foolish men; as free, and not using your liberty for a cloak of maliciousness, but as the servants of God. Honor all men. Love the brotherhood. Fear God. Honor the king. Servants, be subject to your masters with all fear; not only to the good and gentle but also to the perverse." Peter learned submission.

b) Restraint

A second lesson that a man like Peter needed to learn was restraint. The Lord had to put a bit in his mouth and teach him restraint, because he was so unrestrained. For example, when the soldiers came to the garden of Gethsemane to capture Jesus (John 18), Peter grabbed a sword and decided that he would single-handedly fight off approximately five hundred soldiers, the high priests, and all their servants. So, he took a sword and swung at the first person he came to. Now Peter was going for his head, but the man ducked and only lost his ear. The Lord reached over, gave the man a new ear, and told Peter to put away his sword. Jesus had to teach Peter restraint.

Peter learned his lesson. In 1 Peter 2:21-23 he says this: "For even hereunto were ye called, because Christ also suffered for us, leaving us an example, that ye should follow his steps; who did no sin, neither was guile found in his mouth; who, when he was reviled, reviled not again; when he suffered, he threatened not, but committed himself to him that judgeth righteously." Peter learned restraint from Christ, who left His life in the care of God.

c) Humility

Another thing a leader needs to learn is humility. Peter's arrogance was revealed when he told Christ that he would never forsake Him or deny Him—but he did. He learned his lesson, because he writes these words in 1 Peter 5:5*b*: "For God resisteth the proud, and giveth grace to the humble."

d) Sacrifice

Jesus told Peter (in John 21:18-19) that he was going to die as a martyr, and then Peter turned right around and basically said, "Well, what about John? Does he get off the hook?" The Lord then said to Peter, "None of your business. You follow Me!"

Peter learned his lesson of sacrifice so well that he wrote, "If ye be reproached for the name of Christ, happy are ye. . . . if any man suffer as a Christian, let him not be ashamed, but let him glorify God on this behalf. . . . Wherefore, let them that suffer according to the will of God commit the keeping of their souls to him" (1 Pet. 4:14*a*, 16, 19*a*).

e) Love

Leaders tend to be task oriented rather than people oriented and therefore tend to just plow people under. Peter was this way, so he needed to learn love. In John 13, the Lord is washing the disciples' feet, teaching them how to love. But when He comes to Peter, He meets with some resistance. Verses 6-9 detail for us Peter's lesson on love: "Then cometh he to Simon Peter; and Peter saith unto him, Lord, dost thou wash my feet? Jesus answered, and said unto him, What I do thou knowest not now, but thou shalt know hereafter. Peter saith unto him, Thou shalt never wash my feet. Jesus answered him, If I wash thee not, thou hast no part with me. Simon Peter saith unto him, Lord, not my feet only, but also my hands and my head (i.e., "Give me a bath")." Then in verse 34 the Lord said, "A new commandment I give unto you, that ye love one another; as I have loved you, that ye also love one another." Jesus had given all the disciples, but especially Peter, a great lesson on love.

It's evident that Peter learned his lesson on love. In 1 Peter 4:8 he writes: "And above all things have fervent love among yourselves; for love shall cover the multitude of sins."

f) Courage

I think that Peter needed to learn courage. In John 21:18-19, Jesus tells Peter that if he is going to follow Him it will cost him his life. Well, he learned courage. In Acts 4 Peter and John are brought before the Sanhedrin and ordered "not to speak at all nor teach in the name of Jesus" (v. 18). Their courage is seen, however, in their reply: "But Peter and John answered and said unto them, Whether it is right in the sight of God to hearken unto you more than unto God, judge ye. For we cannot but speak the things which we have seen and heard" (vv. 19-20).

One chapter later, in Acts 5, the apostles are again brought before the Sanhedrin for not obeying their order to stop preaching. Again their courage is seen in verse 29 when they reply, "We ought to obey God rather than men."

So, Peter learned submission, restraint, humility, sacrifice, love, and courage from the lessons the Lord gave him.

How did the Lord make a leader? He took someone with the right raw material, put him through the right experiences, gave him the right teaching—and He came out with Peter. Oh, what a leader he was. *His leadership is seen throughout the first twelve chapters of Acts.* He was the one who made the move to replace Judas with Matthias (Acts 1:15-26); he was the spokesman of the church on Pentecost (Acts 2:14-40); he, along with John, healed a lame man (Acts 3:1-11); he, along with John, defied the Sanhedrin (Acts 4:1-22); he dealt with the hypocrisy of Ananias and Sapphira (Acts 5:1-11); he dealt with the problem of Simon the magician (Acts 8:9-25); he healed Aeneas and raised Dorcas from the dead (Acts 9:32-43); he took the gospel to the Gentiles (Acts 10:1—11:18); and he wrote two marvelous epistles in which he repeated all the lessons that Jesus had taught him, thus passing them on to us. What a man he was!

How did it end for him? The unanimous tradition of the early church tells us that Peter was crucified as Christ has predicted he would be. But before he was crucified, he was forced to watch the crucifixion of his wife. It is said that during his wife's crucifixion, he stood at the foot of her cross, continuously encouraging her with the words "Remember the Lord, remember the Lord." After she died, he himself was crucified, but he was crucified upside down at his own request because he said that he was not worthy to die as his Lord.

I believe Peter's life can be summed up in the last words he ever wrote. Second Peter 3:18 is his word to you: "But grow in grace, and in the knowledge of our Lord and Savior, Jesus Christ. To him be glory both now and forever. Amen."

Focusing on the Facts

1. According to Ephesians 4:12, why were the apostles given to the church? What kind of example did they set (see p. 22)?
2. How did the apostles use the gifts of miracles and healings in their ministry (Matt. 10:1)? What did those gifts confirm (see p. 23)?
3. From what group of people did Christ choose the twelve (see p. 24)?
4. How many lists of the apostles are in the Bible? What are the passages (see p. 24)?
5. Why is Peter always mentioned first in the lists of the apostles (see p. 24)?
6. How many groups of apostles are found in the lists? Name the members of each group (see p. 24).
7. Why were the apostles listed in the first group closer to Christ than those in the other groups? What principle does that illustrate (see p. 25)?
8. Who were the leaders in each of the groups of apostles (see pp. 25-26)?
9. Describe the contrast between Peter and John, between Nathanael and Thomas, and between Matthew and Simon the Zealot (see pp. 25-26).
10. In what ways did the Lord deal more with Peter than with any other disciple (see p. 26)?
11. What three elements should make up the raw material of a leader? In what ways did Peter manifest each of those elements (see pp. 27-28)?
12. What was Peter's trade? Where did he live? Was he married? How do we know (see p. 28)?
13. Why did Jesus change Simon's name to Peter (see p. 28)?
14. What reasons did Jesus have for using the name Simon (see pp. 28-29)?

15. When Peter confessed Christ as the Son of God, what experience was God allowing him to have (John 6:67; Matt. 16:15-16)? Why did he need that experience (see p. 30)?
16. In what ways did Peter unlock the kingdom of heaven (see pp. 30-31)?
17. Why did Jesus rebuke Peter in Matthew 16:23? Why is that an important lesson for all leaders to learn (see p. 31)?
18. In what way did Peter reject Christ. (Matt. 26:69-75; see p. 32)?
19. What did Jesus confront Peter with in John 21:15-17 (see p. 32)?
20. Why do leaders need to learn submission? What did Peter learn (1 Pet. 2:13-18; see p. 33)?
21. Why did Peter need to learn restraint (see pp. 33-34)?
22. What did Peter learn about humility (1 Pet. 5:5; see p. 34)?
23. What did Peter learn about sacrifice (1 Pet. 4:14, 16, 19; see p. 34)?
24. Why did Peter need to learn to love? How did Christ teach him about love (John 13:6-9, 34; see pp. 34-35)?
25. Describe how Peter manifested courage (Acts 4:18-20; 5:29; see p. 35).
26. In what ways was Peter's leadership manifested in the first twelve chapters of Acts (see p. 35)?

Pondering the Principles

1. Do you have the right raw material to be a leader? Peter asked many questions of Christ. Do you ask your leaders questions so that you might understand God's truth better? Do you take the initiative like Peter? Do you try to answer spiritual questions yourself rather than letting someone else do it for you? Peter was usually in the middle of whatever action was occurring. Do you want to be involved in what Christ is doing? Even if you don't think that God wants you to be a leader, you should still try to develop those qualities in your life. Make that commitment.
2. What have you learned from the experiences that the Lord has given you? Be specific. Thank God for both the good and bad experiences because they all are important in your growth as a Christian. Based on what your life was like before you became a Christian, how has your life changed? Thank God that right now He is molding you into the person He wants you to be.
3. Peter had to learn several lessons to be a leader. God may or may not be calling you to be a leader, but all the lessons Peter learned are applicable to all Christians. Look up the following verses: Acts 4:19-20; 1 Peter 2:13-18, 21-23; 4:8, 16; 5:5. What can you learn from what Peter learned regarding courage? submission? restraint? love? sacrifice? humility? Ask God to help you apply what you have learned.

3

The Master's Men—Part 1

Outline

Review
I. The Initiation of the Apostles
II. The Impact of the Apostles
III. The Identity of the Apostles
   A. Simon Peter

Lesson
   B. Andrew
      1. His proclamation about Jesus
      2. His position among the apostles
      3. His portrait in John's gospel
         a) The incidental circumstances
            (1) John 1:40-42*a*
            (2) John 6:8-9
            (3) John 12:20-22
         b) The identified characteristics
            (1) His openness
            (2) His faith
            (3) His humility
   C. James the Son of Zebedee
      1. The implications of his title
      2. The incidents of his appearance
         a) Luke 9:51-56
         b) Matthew 20:20-24
         c) Acts 12:1-4*a*
   D. John
      1. His passion misunderstood
      2. His personality discussed
         a) Characterized by love
            (1) His title of love
               (*a*) John 13:23
               (*b*) John 19:26
               (*c*) John 20:2*a*
               (*d*) John 21:7*a*

        (*e*) John 21:20*a*, 24*a*
    (2) His theology of love
        (*a*) God is a God of love
        (*b*) God loved His Son
        (*c*) God loved Christ's disciples
        (*d*) God loves all men
        (*e*) God is loved by Christ
        (*f*) Christ loved the disciples in general
        (*g*) Christ loved individuals
        (*h*) Christ expected all men to love Him
        (*i*) Christ taught that we should love one another
        (*j*) Christ emphasized that love is the fulfilling of the whole law
  b) Characterized by truth
    (1) The witness of John the Baptist
    (2) The witness of Scripture
    (3) The witness of the Father
    (4) The witness of Christ Himself
    (5) The witness of Christ's miracles
    (6) The witness of the Holy Spirit
    (7) The witness of the apostles

Review

As we look at Matthew 10:1-4, we find ourselves getting acquainted with the apostles of our Lord.

I. THE INITIATION OF THE APOSTLES (v. 1*a*; see pp. 8-18)

II. THE IMPACT OF THE APOSTLES (v. 1*b*; see pp. 19, 23)
We are now in the process of looking at:

III. THE IDENTIFICATION OF THE APOSTLES (vv. 2-4)

  A. Simon Peter (see pp. 26-36)

    In our last lesson we noted that the leader of the apostles was Peter. The list of the apostles in verses 2-4 starts out "the first, Simon, who is called Peter." Peter was not the first one called. According to John 1:35-40, John* and Andrew were the first ones converted. The word "first" in verse 2 is the Greek word *prōtos,* which carries the idea of first in the sense of "foremost one," "primary one," or "chief one." This use of *prōtos* is also

*Note: Of the two disciples mentioned in John 1:35-40, only Andrew is specifically named. However, it is generally accepted that the other disciple was John. This is consistent with his practice of never naming himself in his gospel.

seen in 1 Timothy 1:15 where Paul says, "Christ Jesus came into the world to save sinners, of whom I am chief (Gk., *prōtos*)." Peter was the leader—the out-front, up-front man. In our last study, we studied Peter, his leadership ability, and how the Lord refined and developed him into a leader that was useful to Him.

Now, for our present study we're going to look at the remaining three apostles of the first group: Andrew, James, and John. Remember that those in this first group were the most intimate with the Lord, were from the same town, had the same profession, and were the first ones called to follow Him in His ministry (Matt. 4:18-22). As we look at these men, ask yourself these questions: What kind of people can God use? What kind of people can change the world? What kind of people can preach the gospel of the kingdom so that souls are saved? What kind of people does God ordain for His purposes?

Usually, when we think about Peter, Andrew, James, and John, we have a picture of stained-glass saints—men who are on a completely different plane than we are on. These men have a certain aura about them. But frankly, that's really not the way it ought to be. They are very common men with a very uncommon calling. In fact, they are very much like us. As we study them, you will see that they demonstrate the kind of people God uses. See if you can find yourself among them.

We have already seen that God uses people like Simon—impulsive, dynamic, impetuous, strong, initiating, and bold.

Lesson

B. Andrew

Andrew was Peter's brother. His name means "manly." He too was a native of Bethsaida, a little village in Galilee, and, like his brother, Andrew was a fisherman. In fact, in Matthew 4:18-20, we are told he was down at the sea fishing with Peter when Jesus came to them and said, "Follow me, and I will make you fishers of men" (v. 19). They had already met Jesus, believed in Him, and affirmed Him as the Messiah, but they went back to their fishing. Here in Matthew 4, the Lord appeared to them again and called them to permanently follow Him.

1. His proclamation about Jesus

Prior to following Jesus Christ, Andrew had been a pious, godly, God-fearing Jew. He had also been a disciple of John the Baptist. In fact, it was John the Baptist who said to Andrew and John, "Behold the Lamb of God!" (John 1:36).

When they heard that, they immediately followed after Jesus. Verses 38 and 39 tell us, "Then Jesus turned, and saw them following, and saith unto them, What seek ye? They said unto him, Rabbi (which is to say, being interpreted, Master), where dwellest thou? He saith unto them, Come and see. They came and saw where he dwelt, and abode with him that day." After spending that day with the Lamb of God, Andrew went and found his brother, Peter, and the first words from his mouth were the proclamation, "We have found the Messiah" (v. 41*b*). Andrew immediately wanted to share the Messiah with his brother.

2. His position among the apostles

From the very beginning, Andrew was a part of the "intimate four." It's interesting to note, however, that there seems to be an inner circle within the first group. The gospels, on numerous occasions, make reference to Peter, James, and John together. Only once (Mark 13:3) is Andrew mentioned along with those three. He was in the most intimate group but he never quite cracked the inner circle. Nevertheless, he was greatly respected and considered to be intimate with Jesus. This is seen in John 12:20-22. Philip, who was in group two, had some Greeks come to him, requesting to see Jesus. Do you know what Philip did? He took them to Andrew. Why? Because Philip must have thought, "If you want to get to Jesus, all you have to do is get to Andrew." Andrew was intimate with Jesus, and respected by the other apostles, but he wasn't in the innermost circle of intimacy with Christ.

3. His portrait in John's gospel

Andrew isn't mentioned in any detail at all in the gospels of Matthew, Mark, or Luke, but in the gospel of John, Andrew emerges from the background. In each of the three instances that he's mentioned, he's doing the same thing—so it's easy to characterize him.

a) The incidental circumstances

(1) John 1:40-42*a*

"One of the two who heard John speak, and followed him, was Andrew, Simon Peter's brother. He first findeth his own brother, Simon, and saith unto him, We have found the Messiah, which is, being interpreted, the Christ. And he brought him to Jesus." If you want to know how to characterize the life of Andrew, it's very simple: *He was the one who was always bringing people to Jesus.*

(2) John 6:8-9

The second time we see Andrew is in the sixth chapter of John. Jesus had been teaching a vast multitude of people late into the day, and they had begun to get hungry. There wasn't enough food to feed the crowd, but Andrew brought a little boy with five barley crackers and two pickled fish to Jesus. I guess Andrew must have thought the Lord could make a lot out of very little.

(3) John 12:20-22

The third time we meet Andrew is in John 12. Philip had been approached by some Greeks who wanted to see Jesus, so Philip took them to Andrew who, in turn, took them to Jesus.

Andrew was always involved in bringing people to Jesus. He must have understood Jesus well enough to know that there wasn't anybody He didn't want to see, anything He couldn't respond to, or any problem He couldn't solve.

b) The identified characteristics

In these three incidents, several of Andrew's characteristics become clear.

(1) His openness

Andrew knew that their primary mission was to "the lost sheep of the house of Israel" (Matt. 10:6), yet he didn't have any problem bringing Gentiles to Jesus. He probably got this attitude from the Lord, because He had originally revealed His Messiahship to a half-breed Samaritan woman. Andrew was never choked by hyper-Judaism—he had an open heart. As far as Andrew was concerned, there wasn't anybody that Jesus would *not* want to see.

(2) His faith

Andrew had a simple faith. I don't know what he was thinking when he brought those five crackers and two fish to Jesus to feed such a huge crowd. He must have been running around looking for anybody with a lunch. But he must have had tremendous faith to believe that the Lord was able to do much with little. After all, he had seen Jesus make water into wine— why couldn't He make food?

(3) His humility

Andrew probably spent his whole life being known as "Simon's brother" or, later on, "Simon Peter's brother." When he found the Messiah, there might have been a temptation to say, "Boy, I'm not telling Peter. This is my chance to be somebody!" But instead, he immediately ran to tell Peter that he found the Messiah, knowing full well that as soon as Peter entered the group, he would run the group. Why? Because that's how Peter was! But Andrew thought more of the work to be done than who was in charge. He thought more of the cause of the eternal virtue of the kingdom than he did of his personal and petty problems. It's sad to say, but there are some people who won't play in the band unless they can beat the big drum. James and John had a problem with that, didn't they? But not Andrew.

Andrew is the picture of all those who labor quietly in humble places, not with eye service as men pleasers, but as servants of Christ doing the will of God from the heart. Andrew was not a pillar like Peter, James, and John—he was a humbler stone. He was one of those rare people who is willing to take second place and to be in the place of support. He was one of those rare people who doesn't mind being hidden as long as the work is done. Andrew was the kind of man that all leaders depend on—the backbone of every ministry. In fact, the cause of Christ is dependent upon those self-forgetting souls who are content to occupy an obscure place, free from self-seeking ambition.

Daniel McLean, a Scotsman with a special affection for Andrew, the patron saint of Scotland, writes, "Gathering together the traces of character found in Scripture (about Andrew), we have neither the writer of an Epistle, nor the founder of a Church, nor a leading figure in the Apostolic Age, but simply . . . an intimate disciple of Jesus Christ, ever anxious that others should know the spring of spiritual joy and share the blessing he so highly prized. A man of very moderate endowment, who scarcely redeemed his early promise, simple minded and sympathetic, without either dramatic power or heroic spirit, yet with that clinging confidence in Christ that brought him into that inner circle of the Twelve; a man of deep religious feeling with little power of expression, magnetic more than electric, better suited for the quiet walks of life than the stirring thoroughfares. Andrew is the apostle of private life—the disciple of the hearth."

God uses people like Andrew—people who quietly and obscurely bring others to Christ. And God knows that it sometimes takes an Andrew to reach a Peter.

C. James the Son of Zebedee

The third name in the first, most intimate group of apostles is James the son of Zebedee. It's interesting to note that he never appears in any of the gospels apart from his brother John. Also, it's important to note that he's always mentioned before John (i.e., "James and John"). I believe this not only indicates that he was the eldest of the two, but also that he was the leader of this rather dynamic duo. He was the strength, the zeal, the passion.

Now, James and John, along with the other members of this first group of four apostles, were employed as fishermen. They were sons of a man named Zebedee, who apparently was wealthy enough to employ hired servants in his fishing business (cf. Mark 1:20). James fits into this first group because he was likely one of the first ones called. According to John 1, Andrew and John were the first two disciples called, but James, probably because of his relationship to John, was able to work his way into that inner circle of intimacy with Christ.

As we look at the Bible, in terms of specific incidents, James appears more as a silhouette than a photograph. So the image we will wind up with will not contain the fullness of his character. Let's begin with a look at:

1. The implications of his title

The best way to get a good look at James is to consider the special title given to him and his brother John. In Mark 3:17, Jesus calls them Boanerges, which means "sons of thunder." Now if James was the leader of these "sons of thunder," he must have been a passionate, zealous, fervent, wild-eyed, ambitious, aggressive guy. This is supported by the fact that in Acts 12, when Herod decides to vex the church, the first person he goes after was James, chopping off his head. Herod then proceeded to capture Peter—but he only put him in jail. This indicates to me that Peter wasn't as big a problem as James. The simple fact that when both James and Peter were captured, James was killed and Peter was not, says something about the kind of man James must have been.

James was strong and zealous—perhaps the New Testament counterpart of Jehu, who said, "Come with me, and see my zeal for the Lord" (2 Kings 10:16), and then uprooted the house of Ahab, sweeping all the Baal worshipers out of the land. It's also obvious that James made enemies fast. Why? He was the first apostle to be martyred. His enemies got rid of him quickly beause he was a real problem—a thunderous individual. His zeal must have also been fed daily by Christ, who caused the disciples to remember what David wrote in Psalm 69:9, "The zeal of thine house hath eaten me up" (John 2:17). I can just see James, when the Lord took out a whip to clear the temple, saying, "Do it, Lord—give it to them!" James was zealous!

Now zeal is a great virtue. I just love someone who's aggressive and charged up, and wants to get the job done. Unfortunately, very often along with zeal comes a lack of wisdom. Sometimes a zealous person is shooting off at the mouth with his guns blazing before he's really thought anything through. You say, "Can God use somebody like that?" Well, as a matter of fact, He did—and his name was James.

2. The incidents of his appearance

Several incidents stand out in Scripture where James is mentioned. Let's look at them.

a) Luke 9:51-56

"And it came to pass, when the time was come that he should be received up, he steadfastly set his face to go to Jerusalem, and sent messengers before his face; and they went, and entered into a village of the Samaritans, to make ready for him. And they did not receive him, because his face was as though he would go to Jerusalem." Some disciples of our Lord were sent into a Samaritan village to prepare His way and to give them the message that the Messiah was coming. But because of the Samaritan's hatred toward the Jews and their place of worship, Jerusalem, they wouldn't receive Christ into their village. In fact, they probably chased His messengers out with curses and with stones. So these messengers returned to Christ and told Him that the village would not receive Him.

In verse 54, we meet the "sons of thunder." "And when his disciples, James and John, saw this, they said, Lord, wilt thou that we command fire to come down from heaven, and consume them, even as Elijah did?" In other words, "Lord, let's just burn them up!" Obviously, James and John didn't have a great missionary heart. "But he turned and rebuked them, and said, Ye know not what manner of spirit ye are of" (v. 55). In other words, Jesus said, "The spirit that Elijah had doesn't apply now. This is not the time for judgment on an ungodly, heretical nation; this is the time for the proclamation of a New Covenant. You're out of sync, guys! Burning them up isn't the attitude to take right now." Why? "For the Son of man is not come to destroy men's lives, but to save them. And they went to another village" (v. 56).

Jesus rebuked them strongly because they were hateful and intolerant. James had a lot of zeal, but little sensitivity. What kind of evangelist would he make? Yet, I have to admit, there's a touch of nobility in James's zeal. I'm glad that he got mad when the Lord was dishonored. I would hate to have seen him pass by the village without a reaction at all. James was zealous, explosive, fervent, and passionate. He didn't just sit and watch things happen.

b) Matthew 20:20-24

Very often, zealous people are also ambitious, goal-oriented people. This characteristic becomes evident in the following incident: "Then came to him the mother of Zebedee's children with her sons, worshiping him, and desiring a certain thing of him. And he said unto her, What wilt thou? She saith unto him, Grant that these, my two sons, may sit, the one on thy right hand, and the other on the left, in thy kingdom." Jesus directed His reply (verses 22-23) to James and John, rather than their mother, because He knew that they were behind it. They were ambitious and wanted to rise to power in the kingdom. In fact, they wanted the principal places of honor and dignity. Well, this selfish request aroused a spirit of rivalry among the disciples, and in verse 24 it reaches such a fever pitch that in verses 25-28 Jesus has to give them a lecture on what real leadership is all about.

James had zeal and great fervor; and because he knew of the Lord's special interest in him, he felt that he ought to receive an equivalent reward. So the Lord told him, "You'll get a reward, but it won't be what you think. Before you get a throne, you're going to suffer—because the way to the throne is always the way of the cross." Fourteen years later, James was martyred. He wanted a crown—Jesus gave him a cup. He wanted power—Jesus gave him servanthood. He wanted to rule—Jesus gave him a martyr's grave.

c) Acts 12:1-4*a*

This is the one incident in the Bible where James appears without his brother John: "Now about that time Herod, the king, stretched forth his hands to vex certain of the church. And he killed James, the brother of John, with the sword. And because he saw it pleased the Jews, he proceeded further to take Peter also. . . . And when he had apprehended him, he put him in prison."

Notice that when Herod wanted to attack the church, he went right for James. Now apparently, he didn't even think about arresting Peter until he was told that what he did to James pleased the Jews. Primarily, it was James that Herod was after. Why? Because he was a "son of thunder," and filled with zeal, ambition, and strong, intolerant feelings.

What kind of people does God use? Well, He uses great leaders like Peter; quiet, behind-the-scenes, obscure, faithful people like Andrew; and brash, courageous, ambitious, zealous, sometimes loveless, insensitive, selfish people like James. Christ brought James's temper under control, bridled his tongue, directed his zeal, and taught him to seek no revenge and desire no honor for himself—and God used him.

The tragedy of zeal without sensitivity

A lack of sensitivity can destroy a ministry. Unfortunately, there are many men who are trying to serve Christ but are utterly insensitive to their congregations, to their families, and to the people around them. One such man was a Norwegian pastor by the name of Henrik Ibsen. His motto was "All or nothing!" and as he preached he hurled out lightning and screamed thunder on his congregation. He was stern, strong, powerful, uncompromising—and utterly insensitive. It was said that the people in his church didn't care for him because he didn't care for them. He was so zealous and ambitious to advance the kingdom and uphold the standard of God, that he was blind to everything else—even his own family.

He had a tiny little girl who was ill, and the doctor told him that if he didn't take her out of the cold Norwegian air to a warmer climate, she would die. Well, he told the doctor, "All or nothing!" and would not leave—so his little girl died. After she died, the mother became so grief-striken that she would sit for hours, holding and fondling the clothes of her little girl, feeding her love-starved heart with empty garments.

This only continued for a few days, because when Henrik saw what she was doing, he took all of the little girl's clothes and gave them to a poor woman in the street. His wife, however, tucked a little bonnet underneath her, which she kept as the last vestige of a memory. But eventually, he found it, gave it away, and gave her a speech about "All or nothing." In just a matter of months, she too died—of grief.

What stupid insensitivity! Unmellowed zeal can only end up in tragedy. I think of the great evangelist, Billy Sunday. All of his children died in unbelief. Was he insensitive to the ones around him while he was winning the world? There are many pastors, evangelists, and Christian people who aren't even listening to what's going on in their own homes. They are so oriented to the task that they neglect the people. Zeal with insensitivity is so cruel. James had to be refined. He had to get from the place where he said, "Just burn them up, Lord, if they don't cooperate," to the place where he cared about people.

What kind of people does God use? What kind of people fit into His plan? Dynamic people like Peter, humble people like Andrew, zealous people like James, and completing the first, most intimate group of apostles:

D. John

1. His passion misunderstood

Usually, when people think about John, they think of someone meek, mild, pale-skinned, and effeminate, lying around with his head on Jesus' shoulder, looking up at Him with a dove-eyed stare. If this is your image of John, you've missed it! He was in all of the incidents about James that we just looked at. He was one of the "sons of thunder." He too was intolerant, ambitious, zealous, and explosive—but not quite as much as James. James seems to be the prominent one in the duo, but John certainly had similar characteristics.

A Negative Quality Made Positive

It's interesting to note that the only time John's name appears alone in the gospels, he's mad at somebody. In Mark 9, we find John mad at someone who was casting out demons. In verse 38, John said to Jesus, "Master, we saw one casting out demons in thy name, and he followeth not us; and we forbade him, because he followeth not us." In other words,

48

John said, "Lord, I told him to be quiet because he wasn't in our group." John was mad at the man casting out demons because he wasn't one of the twelve!

John was sectarian, narrow-minded, unbending, and ridiculously intolerant, but those characteristics became a strength in his character because he had a tremendous capacity for love. Someone who has a great capacity for love but has no sense of the truth, no limits, no guidelines, and no strong convictions becomes a disaster of tolerance and sentimentality. It's obvious that God chose John to be the greatest New Testament writer concerning love and truth because he was strong and uncompromising. Otherwise, love would have been turned into sentimentalism. Also, for someone to speak the truth in love, he has to be as much committed to the truth as he is to love, and John was committed to both.

2. His personality discussed

Two words characterize John's life and teaching: love and witness. He uses the word *love* more than eighty times, and the word *witness,* in one form or another, almost seventy times. John was the witness to the truth and the teacher of love—the personification of speaking the truth in love. He was the truth-seeker, the discoverer, the visionary; and the reason he is seen leaning on Christ's breast was not because of some sloppy sentimentalism, it was because his heart literally hungered for the truth and because of his deep affection for Christ. He wanted to gather every word that came out of the Lord's lips as well as bask in the light of His love.

John became a lover, but a lover whose love was controlled by the truth. His control was born out of the tremendous zeal, passion, and strength that was in his fiery character. Read 1, 2, and 3 John and see how he denounces the antichrists who stand up in the church to twist and pervert God's Word. He's firm and strong. Read the gospel of John and see how he contrasts the people of God with the people of Satan—the redeemed against the lost—the righteous against the unrighteous. John knew where the lines were drawn, so his love never turned into sentimentalism.

a) Characterized by love

(1) His title of love

We don't see much about John in the other gospels, unless it's with James. But in his own gospel, he appears several times—always the same way.

(*a*) John 13:23—"Now there was leaning on Jesus' bosom one of his disciples, whom Jesus loved." Throughout his gospel, John never uses his name. He just refers to himself as the disciple "whom Jesus loved."

(*b*) John 19:26—"When Jesus, therefore, saw his mother, and the disciple standing by, whom he loved, he saith unto his mother, Woman, behold thy son!"

(*c*) John 20:2*a*—"Then she runneth, and cometh to Simon Peter, and to the other disciple, whom Jesus loved."

(*d*) John 21:7*a*—"Therefore, that disciple whom Jesus loved saith unto Peter, It is the Lord."

(*e*) John 21:20*a*, 24*a*—"Then Peter, turning about, seeth the disciple whom Jesus loved, following; who also leaned on his breast at supper. . . . This is the disciple who testifieth of these things, and wrote these things." In other words, it was "the disciple whom Jesus loved" who wrote the gospel of John.

John was literally in awe that Jesus loved him. He wasn't being proud or boastful, having the perspective, "Oh, the Lord loves me so much because I'm so wonderful. I just want you to know that I'm the disciple that Jesus loved." Actually, his perspective was just the opposite. He was amazed that Jesus loved the one who wanted to burn up all the Samaritans, and who wanted the place of honor in the kingdom that he didn't even deserve. John's reference to himself as "the disciple whom Jesus loved" was basically his way of emphasizing God's grace in his life.

There was something special about John. Jesus never had to ask John if he loved Him—but He did have to ask Peter (John 21:15-17). Jesus never had to ask John to follow Him—but he did have to ask Peter (John 21:22). And when it came down to passing out the work, He said to Peter, "Feed my sheep" (John 21:16-17), but He told John to take care of His mother (John 19:26-27). Tradition tells us that John never left the city of Jerusalem until Mary, the mother of Jesus, died, thus keeping his vow to the Lord.

(2) His theology of love

John's theology of love can be summarized into ten statements.

(*a*) God is a God of love (John 5:42; 15:10).

(*b*) God loved His Son (John 10:17; 15:9; 17:23-24, 26).

(*c*) God loved Christ's disciples (John 16:27; 17:23).

(*d*) God loves all men (John 3:16).

(*e*) God is loved by Christ (John 14:31).

(*f*) Christ loved the disciples in general (John 13:1-34; 14:21; 15:9-10).

(*g*) Christ loved individuals (John 11:5, 36; 13:23).

(*h*) Christ expected all men to love Him (John 8:42; 14:23).

(*i*) Christ taught that we should love one another (John 13:34-35; 15:12-13).

(*j*) Christ emphasized that love is the fulfilling of the whole law (John 15:10; 1 John 3:23-24).

b) Characterized by truth

Another important aspect of John's character was his clear perception of truth. He uses the word *witness* thirty times, and its cognate words *record* and *testify* (or *testimony*) thirteen and twenty-five times respectively. He was constantly affirming the witness of the truth.

(1) The witness of John the Baptist (John 5:32-33)

(2) The witness of Scripture (John 5:39)

(3) The witness of the Father (John 5:37)

(4) The witness of Christ Himself (John 8:14)

(5) The witness of Christ's miracles (John 5:36)

(6) The witness of the Holy Spirit (John 15:26)

(7) The witness of the apostles (John 15:27)

John was always speaking the truth in love. He was a fiery lover whose love was a passionate devotion to the truth.

What kind of people does God use? What kind of people did Christ draw into intimacy with Him? When the God of the universe—the living, eternal, almighty, holy God—walked in this world, what were the four men who became His intimates like? One was a dynamic, strong, bold leader like Peter who took charge, initiated, planned, strategized, confronted, and commanded people to Christ. Another was a humble, gentle, inconspicuous man like Andrew, who saw people as individuals, not crowds, and while he never attracted a mob, he kept bringing people to Jesus. The Lord also picked a zealous, passionate, uncompromising, insensitive, ambitious man like James, who could see a goal and strive for it with all his might, even if he died in the process. And then there was sensitive, loving, believing, intimate John, who sought the truth and then spoke the truth in love so that he attracted people to Christ. The Lord made these men fishers of men, in spite of what they were.

As we saw in our last lesson, Peter was finally crucified upside down at his own request—unwavering in his faith in Christ (see p. 36).

Tradition tells us that Andrew had the privilege of preaching in a province in which the governor's wife received Jesus Christ as her Savior. The governor was so upset, he demanded that his wife reject Christ. When she refused, he crucified Andrew on an X-shaped cross. Andrew hung alive on that cross for two days, and in the midst of his agony he continued to preach the gospel of Christ—still trying to bring people to Jesus.

Tradition also tells us that the officer who guarded James on his way to being beheaded by the Roman sword, was so impressed with James's courage and constant zeal, that he fell down at the apostle's feet and begged pardon for the part he had played in the rough treatment he had received. James lifted the man up, embraced and kissed him, and said, "Peace, my son; peace be to thee, and the pardon of thy faults." Immediately transformed, the officer publically confessed his surrender to Christ and was beheaded alongside James.

John, who was banished to the isle of Patmos after a long life, died around 98 A.D. during the reign of Trajan. Those who knew him best said their remembrance of John was a phrase that he constantly used: "My little children, love one another."

What kind of people does God use? Ordinary people—with all the struggles, all the strengths, and all the weaknesses of people like us. *It's not what you are that's important, the issue is what you are willing to become.* The fishermen of Galilee became fishers of men on a tremendous scale, gathering many souls into the church. In a sense, they're still casting their nets into the sea of the world—by their testimony of Jesus in the gospels and in the epistles. They are still bringing multitudes to become disciples of Him among whose first followers they had the privilege to be numbered. Christ took very common men and made them into very uncommon apostles, and He can do a similar work in our lives too.

Focusing on the Facts

1. Why was Peter considered the "first" apostle (Matt. 10:2; see pp. 39-40)?
2. Who were the first four disciples Jesus called into ministry (Matt. 4:18-22; see p. 40)?
3. Who was Andrew? Where did he come from (see p. 40)?
4. What was Andrew like before he followed Jesus? What did he do after he met Jesus (John 1:41; see pp. 40-41)?
5. When some Greeks wanted to see Jesus, why did Philip take them to see Andrew (John 12:20-22; see p. 41)?
6. Based on incidents recorded in John's gospel, how can you characterize Andrew (John 1:40-42; 6:8-9; 12:20-22; see pp. 41-42)?
7. Describe Andrew's open heart, faith, and humility. What kind of servant was Andrew (see pp. 42-43)?
8. Why is James always mentioned before John (see p. 44)?
9. What was the title that Jesus gave to both James and John? What did it mean (see p. 44)?
10. Describe the character of James (see p. 44-45).
11. What characteristic often accompanies zeal? Can God use a man like that (see p. 45)?
12. What was the reaction of James and John when a Samaritan village wouldn't receive Jesus (Luke 9:54)? How did Jesus respond to them (Luke 9:55-56; see pp. 45-46)?
13. According to Jesus, what had to happen to James before he could get a throne (Matt. 20:22-23; see p. 46)?
14. How did James die? Why did Herod seek to have James killed first (Acts 12:1-2; see p. 47)?
15. What can destroy a ministry? Describe how it can (see pp. 47-48).
16. What characteristics of John became his strength when they were combined with his great capacity for love? What happens to one who loves without those characteristics (see p. 49)?
17. What two words characterize John's life and teaching? Explain (see p. 49).
18. How did John describe himself in his gospel? What was he emphasizing by using that title (e.g., John 13:23; see p. 50)?
19. What are the ten statements of John's theology of love (see p. 51)?
20. Give some examples of the witness to the truth that John recorded (see p. 51).
21. According to tradition, how did Peter, Andrew, James, and John die (see pp. 52)?

22. Complete this statement: "It's not what you are that's important; the issue is what you are _____ _____ _____ " (see p. 52).

Pondering the Principles

1. Andrew revealed three of the important qualities of the servant of God: an open heart, faith, and humility. On a scale of 1-10, rate your spiritual maturity in each of those qualities. What do you need to do to open your heart more to those who don't know Christ? How can you improve your faith in God's ability to meet the little needs in your life? What do you need to do to be more humble in your support of your leaders? Not everyone can be a leader like Peter, but everyone can be a faithful servant like Andrew. Strive to be like him.
2. Since a lack of sensitivity can destroy a ministry, examine the ministry you're involved in. Are you sensitive to the people you serve with? Are you sensitive to your family? When your ministry takes you away from them, do you try to make that up to them? Are you sensitive to the leading of the Lord, or do you make decisions in your ministry without consulting Him? If you are lacking sensitivity to any of those people, then you need to confess that to them. Ask God to give you a greater sensitivity from now on.
3. Is your love controlled by truth? Do find that you are tolerant, even to the point that you compromise the truth? Read Ephesians 4:15 and 4:25. What kind of commitment to truth and love do you need to have to fulfill those verses? Only as you are willing to make that commitment will you be able to stand firm as a witness for Christ in the world. Begin to stand by making that commitment today.

4

The Master's Men—Part 2

Outline

Introduction

Review
I. The Initiation of the Apostles
II. The Impact of the Apostles
III. The Identity of the Apostles
  A. Simon Peter
  B. Andrew
  C. James the Son of Zebedee
  D. John

Lesson
  E. Philip
    1. His position among the twelve
    2. His portrayal from John's gospel
      a) John 1:43-46
        (1) The account described
        (2) The attributes distinguished
      b) John 6:5-7
        (1) The account described
        (2) The attributes distinguished
      c) John 12:20-22
        (1) The account described
        (2) The attributes distinguished
      d) John 14:8-11
        (1) The account described
        (2) The attributes distinguished
  F. Bartholomew (Nathanael)
    1. His study of Scripture
    2. His sin of prejudice
    3. His sincerity of heart
    4. His search for truth exposed
    5. His statement of faith
    6. His special insight into Jesus' power

Introduction

What kind of people does God use for His purposes? What kind of men did Jesus choose? Well, when most people think of the twelve apostles, they are prone to think of stained-glass saints, men without faults, men who manifested none of the failures that beset the rest of humanity. But if you look at the apostles that way, you're wrong! They were people just like all of us. Even though they were specially called, specially transformed, specially trained, and specially sent by Christ—they were people just like us.

We live in a very qualification-conscious society. There are qualifications for just about everything. For example, we have to qualify to buy a house, to buy a car, to get a credit card, to apply for a job, to pursue a career, to enroll in school, to train for a particular skill, to join a team—or whatever else we want to do. It seems everything we do requires that we qualify. Somebody establishes standards that we have to meet because society has determined that it's only going to use qualified people.

Now what qualifications does God have? What does God require of those who serve Him? What kind of people does Jesus use in His ministry to advance His eternal kingdom? Well, since nobody is qualified, God has only one alternative—to use the unqualified to do the impossible. That is essentially how God works. God uses unqualified people, moves into their lives and with saving, sanctifying grace, and transforms them into useful instruments to perform His purposes. Let's look at some biblical examples of unqualified people that God has used.

1. *Noah* got drunk and conducted himself in a lewd way.

2. *Abraham* doubted God, lied about his wife, and committed adultery.

3. *Isaac* sinned as his father had taught him, lying about his wife Rebekah to Abimelech.

4. *Jacob* extorted the birthright from Esau, deceived his father, and raised a family of immoral children.

5. *Joseph* was an outcast and hated by his brothers.

6. *Moses* was a murderer and, acting in pride, tried to steal God's glory by striking a rock to get water from it, instead of obediently speaking to it as God had told him to do.

7. *Aaron,* the high priest, led Israel in the worship of the golden calf and the accompanying orgy.

8. *Joshua* was so deceived by the Gibeonites that he made a treaty with them instead of destroying them as God had told him to do, and because of his disobedience, Israel was troubled endlessly by them.

9. *Gideon* had no confidence in himself and even less confidence in God's plan and power.

10. *Samson* was marked as a man with a lustful love for a wretched woman.

11. *Ruth* was in the messianic line, yet she was an accursed Moabitess.

12. *Samuel* was only a little child when he began to serve God.

13. *David* was a ladies' man, an adulterer, a murderer, a poor father, and a man with such bloody hands that God wouldn't even let him build the Temple.

14. *Solomon* was the world's leading polygamist.

15. *Isaiah* put his trust in a human king.

16. *Ezekiel* was a brash, tough, strong-minded, crusty, say-what-you-think priest.

17. *Daniel* was educated in a pagan country and taught the wisdom of the bitter and hasty Chaldeans.

18. *Hosea* married a prostitute.

19. *Jonah* defied God in direct disobedience and got terribly upset when the Gentile city of Nineveh was converted.

20. *Habakkuk* questioned the divine plan.

21. *Elijah* was able to handle 850 false priests and prophets, but ran like a maniac from one woman—Jezebel.

22. *Paul* was a former Christian killer.

23. *Timothy* was ashamed of Christ and had to be rebuked by Paul.

If you'll just follow the flow of the people God used, you'll see a march of the unqualified. God uses unqualified people! And when you look at the twelve, you'll meet a group of unqualified men, just like all the rest.

Review

We have been studying Matthew 10:2-4 and identifying the twelve apostles. We have already discussed the first four and have seen that they were very much like us. What kind of people are qualified for the Lord's work? Let's briefly review the characteristics of the first four apostles that we have already studied, to remind us of the kind of people Jesus uses.

I. THE INITIATION OF THE APOSTLES

II. THE IMPACT OF THE APOSTLES

III. THE IDENTITY OF THE APOSTLES

A. Simon Peter

Jesus uses dynamic, strong, bold leaders like Peter, who take charge, initiate, plan, strategize, confront, rebuke, and command people to Christ, leaders who talk a better game than they play and often act too hastily, but are usually eager to be forgiven and restored (see pp. 26-36).

B. Andrew

Our Lord also uses humble, gentle, inconspicuous, quiet souls like Andrew, who seek no prominence and never preach to crowds, but quietly bring individuals to Christ (see pp. 40-44).

C. James the Son of Zebedee

Jesus also uses zealous, passionate, uncompromising, task-oriented, insensitive, ambitious dynamos like James, who wind up getting killed because nobody can handle them. These people see a job to do and will die getting it done (see pp. 44-48).

D. John

He also uses sensitive, loving, believing, intimate, truth-seekers like John, who speak the truth in love and attract men to Christ (see pp. 48-53).

Now, those four men made up the first, most intimate group of apostles. If you remember, we saw that the twelve were organized into three groups of four members each, and each group was in a decreasing level of intimacy with Christ (see pp. 24-25). Now that we have seen those who were the most intimate to Christ, let's continue on to group two.

Lesson

E. Philip

This is Philip the disciple—not to be confused with Philip the deacon in Acts 6 who later became an evangelist. The name *Philip* is a Greek name which means "lover of horses." Now all of the twelve were Jews, so Philip also had a Jewish name (we just don't know what it was), but for some reason, Philip always went by his Greek name. It's interesting to note that when some Greeks wanted to see Jesus (John 12:20-22), they went to Philip. Since his name was Greek, it's possible that he became the person the Greeks went to if they wanted to see Jesus.

1. His position among the twelve

In all the lists of the twelve apostles, Philip is always mentioned at the beginning of the second group. This seems to indicate that he was the leader of group two, which included Bartholomew, Thomas, and Matthew.

According to John 1:44, "Philip was of Bethsaida, the city of Andrew and Peter." In all probability, Philip had grown up with Andrew and Peter, and was perhaps a close friend of theirs. In fact, there were probably friendships established between Peter, Andrew, James, John, Philip, Bartholomew, and Thomas prior to their discipleship since they, most likely, were all fishermen from Galilee. (cf. John 21:2—Note: the "two others of his disciples" not named in John 21:2 are most commonly believed to be Andrew and Philip because they are the ones most frequently associated with the disciples who *are* named.)

2. His portrayal from John's gospel

The first three gospels don't tell us anything about Philip, they only give his name. But John's gospel mentions him four times, giving us an opportunity to get to know him. Let's look at these four different accounts and meet Philip.

a) John 1:43-46

(1) The account described

"The day following [the day after Peter and Andrew encountered Christ] Jesus would go forth into Galilee, and findeth Philip, and saith unto him, Follow me." This is the first direct call of a disciple. Peter and Andrew had already met Christ, but they had sought Him out. Philip is the first individual to whom the Lord expressly said, "Follow me."

Verse 43 tells us that Jesus found Philip. May I hasten to add that Philip had a seeking heart. This is evident from verse 45: "Philip findeth Nathanael, and saith unto him, We have found him, of whom Moses in the law, and the prophets, did write, Jesus of Nazareth, the son of Joseph." Apparently, Philip and Nathanael had been studying the law and the prophets and were seeking for the Messiah. So, when Jesus came to Philip and said, "Follow me," his eyes, ears, and heart were open and ready to follow Him.

Did Jesus find Philip or did Philip find Jesus?

In John 1:43 it says that Jesus found Philip, but in verse 45, Philip tells Nathanael that he found Jesus. Well, from the Lord's viewpoint, He found Philip; but from Philip's viewpoint, he found the Lord. Isn't that the way your own testimony goes? The sovereign side is that God found you, but the human side is that you found God. When salvation occurred, both you and God were seeking. Jesus said, "For the Son of man is come to seek and to save that which was lost" (Luke 19:10), but God also says, in Jeremiah 29:13, "And ye shall seek me, and find me, when ye shall search for me with all your heart." God seeks the true heart that seeks Him, and this is illustrated in the call of Philip. Jesus found him, but He found a man who was honestly seeking the truth.

At the beginning of verse 45 we see Philip's immediate response to his own conversion: "Philip findeth Nathanael." He immediately ran to tell Nathanael that he had found the Messiah. You can just imagine the excitement, the thrill, the joy, and the ecstasy that he had in telling Nathanael that the One they had been searching for had arrived. In fact, the end of verse 46 tells us that he wanted Nathanael to go and see Him for himself.

(2) The attributes distinguished

What do we learn about Philip from this account in John 1:43-46? The first thing we learn about him is that he was a truly religious, God-fearing Jew who was honestly seeking for the Messiah. We also learn that his immediate response to his own salvation was evangelism. He immediately went to his friend, Nathanael, and told him of Christ. So, Philip had a seeking heart and the heart of an evangelist.

Friendship Evangelism

I'm convinced that friendships provide the most fertile soil for evangelism. That is because the reality of Christ is introduced into a relationship of love that has already been established. Invariably, when somebody becomes a Christian, their first reaction to the warmth and joy of their newfound life is to find a friend and tell him what has happened. Unfortunately, many Christians lose this initial desire to share their faith in Christ with their friends. And when that happens, it's a sad commentary on one of two things—either they don't have any unsaved friends, or they don't care anymore. Both are tragic!

b) John 6:5-7

(1) The account described

As we come to John 6, it's important to remember that Philip had seen Jesus make water into wine (John 2:1-11) as well as many other demonstrations of His supernatural power. In fact, Jesus had just spent the entire day teaching and healing the diseases of a crowd of 5,000 men and at least 25,000 women and children. As evening approached, this massive crowd began to get hungry. With that as a background, look at verse 5: "When Jesus then lifted up his eyes, and saw a great company come unto him, he saith unto Philip, Where shall we buy bread, that these may eat?"

Now, *why did Jesus single Philip out?* I believe that Philip was in charge of the food. We know that Judas was in charge of the money, so it's reasonable to assume that somebody was in charge of the food. Somebody had to figure out how much food was needed, where it would be purchased or acquired, and how it would be rationed and distributed as they traveled around and ministered. It seems to me that this was Philip's area of responsibility. So the Lord said, "Philip, how are we going to get the bread to feed these folks?"

You say, "Well, why did He ask him that?" Verse 6 tells us why: "And this he said to test him; for he himself knew what he would do." Jesus knew that He was going to feed them miraculously, but He was testing Philip. In other words, He was saying, "Now Philip, you've seen Me make water into wine. Since we don't have enough food for this multitude, what would you suggest?"

In verse 7, Philip replies, "Two hundred denarii's worth of bread is not sufficient for them, that every one of them may take a little." The fact that Philip gave Jesus an instant answer proves to me that Philip was, indeed, responsible for the food. He had already analyzed it, figured it out, and calculated that two hundred denarii would not be enough money to feed the crowd. This figure was either the amount Philip calculated they could gather from the people or the amount the disciples had available to spend on food. And the reason two hundred denarii wouldn't be enough is because one denarius (a day's wage) only bought thirty-six barley biscuits, each of which was about the size of a hand, one and one-half inches thick. So, when Jesus asked Philip how they were going to feed the crowd, we see that he had already figured out that 7,200 barley biscuits wouldn't be enough to go around.

(2) The attributes distinguished

It's interesting that it never entered into Philip's mind that the Lord was supernatural and that He could do a creative miracle. *The supernatural resources of Jesus Christ totally escaped his thinking*—he just calculated everything out. Philip was analytical, pragmatic, and pessimistic. He's the kind of person who would sit in a board meeting, punch all the figures into his calculator, and say, "Can't do it! We don't have the money! It can't be done!" He had too much arithmetic to be adventurous and was so stuck on facts that he missed faith altogether.

Christ was trying to teach Philip about faith and that with Him all things were possible, but he was such a thick-headed character, he wasn't learning the lesson. When the Lord asked Philip where they were going to buy the bread to feed the crowd, he should have answered, "Lord, You made wine at Cana and You fed Your children manna in the wilderness—do what You want. You have the power to make food to feed them." It's interesting that Jesus had been healing all day long and Philip had been watching the demonstration of His supernatural power. But he still said, "It can't be done!"

Philip was a materialist—a man of practical, common-sense measurements. He was methodical and mechanical, with very little understanding of the supernatural. He was a facts-and-figures guy, always going by what appeared on the human level.

c) John 12:20-22

    (1) The account described

"And there were certain Greeks among them that came up to worship at the feast" (v. 20). Now, these were God-fearing Greeks who had come to Jerusalem to celebrate the Passover. "The same came, therefore, to Philip, who was of Bethsaida, of Galilee, and desired him, saying, Sir, we would see Jesus" (v. 21). These Greeks devotees of Judaism heard about Christ and wanted to see Him, so they went to Philip to arrange a meeting. Now the reason they went to him was probably because of his Greek name.

Well, Philip may have been an approachable, warmhearted fellow, but he didn't take these Greeks to Jesus. Verse 22 says, "Philip cometh and telleth Andrew; and again Andrew and Philip tell Jesus." In other words, Philip said, "Now you guys wait here. I don't know if I can let you see Jesus, so let me check first," and he went and told Andrew.

    (2) The attributes distinguished

This incident shows us that Philip was neither decisive nor forceful. Peter would have grabbed those Gentiles, dragged them into the presence of Jesus, and said, "Lord, here are some Greeks who want to see You." But not Philip—he had to check it out with somebody else first!

Do you know what was bothering Philip? He was still living under Jesus' command "Go not into the way of the Gentiles . . . but go, rather, to the lost sheep of the house of Israel" (Matt. 10:5*b*, 6). Philip didn't know if Jesus would see these Gentiles because he was always going strictly by the book. *His vision was so narrow that he missed the message of grace.* Yes, Jesus did come to the lost sheep of the house of Israel, but He also said, John 6:37, "All that the Father giveth me shall come to me; and him that cometh to me I will in no wise cast out." Unfortunately, Philip lacked the power to see beyond the specifics to the spirit of grace. He was always going by the book and analyzing everything, so consequently, he missed the full perspective of the purpose of Christ.

d) John 14:8-11

    (1) The account described

> The setting in John 14 is the upper room on the night of the final Passover Supper. Jesus was unfolding His heart to His disciples since He knew that He was about to be betrayed arrested, and crucified. Everything was coming to an end. In verse 8, Philip enters the narrative and says, "Lord, show us the Father, and it sufficeth us." Look at Jesus' reply: "Jesus saith unto him, Have I been such a long time with you, and yet hast thou not known me, Philip? He that hath seen me hath seen the Father; and how sayest thou then, Show us the Father? Believest thou not that I am in the Father, and the Father in me? The words that I speak unto you, I speak not of myself; but the Father that dwelleth in me, he doeth the works. Believe me that I am in the Father, and the Father in me; or else believe me for the very works' sake" (vv. 9-11).

    (2) The attributes distinguished

> For three years Philip had gazed into the only face of God men ever saw—and he said, "Show us the Father." His spiritual vision was unclear and his faith was weak. Somehow, the fact that Jesus was God didn't register in Philip's mind. He was ignorant, slow of heart, skeptical, and unconvinced.

The gospel of John shows us that Philip had a seeking heart and an evangelistic heart. But it also shows us that he was a man of limited ability, inadequate faith, and imperfect understanding, a man who fooled around with facts and figures, but missed the big picture of Christ's power and grace. Philip's faith was limited by money, circumstances, and proof. He was pessimistic, reluctant, insecure, unsure, analytical, and skeptical—yet the Lord used him. In fact, someday he's going to reign over the tribes of Israel in the kingdom.

Tradition tells us that Philip wound up dying as a martyr because he wouldn't deny Christ. He was stripped naked, hung upside down by his feet, and pierced in his ankles and thighs so that he would slowly bleed to death. He had only one request: that his dead body would not be wrapped in linen like the body of his Lord—because he wasn't worthy of that.

I'm glad that God can use the slow, faithless, analytical skeptics. Why? Because many of us find ourselves in that category, don't we?

F. Bartholomew (Nathanael)

The next individual listed in the second group of apostles, here in Matthew 10:3, is Bartholomew. Actually, his last name was Bartholomew and his first name was Nathanael. So, his full name was Nathanael Bartholomew. *Nathanael* means "gift of God," and *Bartholomew* means "son of Tolmai."

As we will soon see, Nathanael was very different from his friend Philip. He was full of faith, contemplative, meditative, and very much in awe of the supernatural. And unlike with Philip, everything was crystal clear to him right from the very beginning.

Nathanael was from Cana of Galilee (John 21:2) and was brought to Jesus by Philip, so he was probably acquainted with the other apostles from Galilee. Only one passage in the Bible really tells us anything about him—John 1:45-51.

1. His study of Scripture (v. 45)

"Philip findeth Nathanael, and saith unto him, We have found him, of whom Moses in the law, and the prophets, did write, Jesus of Nazareth, the son of Joseph."

The way that Philip approached Nathanael implies that Nathanael was a searcher of Scripture and a seeker of divine truth. He also must have had a knowledge of messianic prophecy. When Philip found Nathanael he basically said, "We've found the One Scripture told us about!" This not only implies that Nathanael was a student of Scripture but that he and Philip had probably spent hours studying the Old Testament together and looking for the Messiah.

So the first thing we learn about Nathanael is that he was a student of Scripture, a searcher of truth, and a seeker of God. Together, he and Philip hungered to know God's truth and looked for the Messiah. However, verse 46 tells us that he had a weakness in his character.

2. His sin of prejudice (v. 46)

"And Nathanael said unto him, Can any good thing come out of Nazareth?"

Nathanael was from Cana, which was even more obscure than Nazareth. But it's very possible that the people from

Nazareth were much more unrefined, wild, and uneducated than the people of Cana. Nazareth was the last stop before the Gentile world—it was out on the fringe. And I'm sure, from Nathanael's perspective, the only thing that ever came out of Nazareth was trouble.

Well, I don't know whether Cana and Nazareth had some kind of competition between them or not, but for whatever reason, Nathanael was guilty of the ugly sin of prejudice. He revealed that he had prejudice toward the town of Nazareth. Do you know what prejudice is? *Prejudice is an uncalled-for generalization based on feelings of superiority.* He just blanketed the whole town of Nazareth and said, "Nothing good could possibly ever come out of there."

Prejudice is ugly—it has stopped many people from hearing the truth of the gospel. In fact, it was prejudice that prevented the scribes and the Pharisees from responding to Jesus Christ, because He wasn't from Jerusalem and He wasn't trained in their schools. They said of the apostles, in Acts, "What do they know? They're ignorant, unlearned, Galilean hayseeds from the North" (cf. Acts 2:7; 4:13). Prejudice is a device often used by Satan to blind people to the truth—and it showed its ugly head in Nathanael.

Fortunately, his prejudice wasn't too deep. At the end of verse 46 when Philip said to him, "Come and see," he went. He could have told Philip, "Not on your life! I wouldn't go near someone from that place!" But he didn't respond that way. His seeking heart overpowered his prejudice.

3. His sincerity of heart (v. 47)

"Jesus saw Nathanael coming to him, and saith of him, Behold an Israelite indeed, in whom is no guile!"

Now that was quite a statement that He made about Nathanael. Jesus called him "an Israelite indeed" because he was a true Jew. You say, *"Can someone be a Jew but not a true Jew?"* Yes! Romans 2:28-29*a* says, "For he is not a Jew who is one outwardly; neither is that circumcision which is outward in the flesh; but he is a Jew who is one inwardly; and circumcision is that of the heart." Also, Romans 9:6*b* says, "For they are not all Israel, who are of Israel." There are Jews in the flesh who are not Jews in the covenant because they do not believe. Nathanael was a true Jew—a God-fearing, God-seeking, Messiah-oriented Jew.

Jesus also said of Nathanael, "in whom is no guile!" In other words, he had no hypocrisy or deceit. He was an honest, sincere Jew who sought after God. But even a man as good as this was stained with the sin of prejudice. The Lord was always working with men who were unqualified at one point or another—even the best of them.

4. His search for truth exposed (v. 48)

"Nathanael saith unto him, How knowest thou me? Jesus answered and said unto him, Before Philip called thee, when thou was under the fig tree, I saw thee."

To further prove how really sincere Nathanael was, when Jesus referred to him as a true Jew without hypocrisy, Nathanael's immediate response was, "How do You know my heart?" In other words, Nathanael knew that he was a sincere God-fearing Jew; he just didn't know how Jesus could possibly know that. But when Jesus demonstrated His omniscience, Nathanael immediately knew that Jesus was the Messiah he'd been searching for.

You say, *"What's the significance of Nathanael being under a fig tree?"* Well, fig trees grew to a height of fifteen feet and would spread their branches as far as twenty-five feet. So, many people in Palestine would plant fig trees next to their houses to provide shade as well as an outdoor shelter. Since many of the houses only had one room, the fig tree became the only place where one could get away from the hustle and bustle indoors. Because of this, it became a place of retreat, a place of respite, and a place to be alone; a place of prayer, meditation, and contemplation; and a place of communing with God, and searching the Scriptures. It may well have been that Nathanael was out under the fig tree meditating, praying, and seeking God in the quietness and solitude of its shade.

So in effect, Jesus says to him in verse 48, "Nathanael, I saw you studying, meditating, and praying in the quiet solitude you had under your fig tree. And I also saw your open heart and your true desire to find the Messiah. Well, here I am!" That was all Nathanael needed to hear.

5. His statement of faith (v. 49)

"Nathanael answered, and saith unto him, Rabbi, thou art the Son of God; thou art the King of Israel."

Nathanael immediately knew who Jesus was. By way of contrast, Philip wasn't sure of His deity even after he was with

Him for three years. Philip knew He was the One Moses spoke about, but he wasn't too sure who He was. Nathanael, on the other hand, knew instantly that Jesus was the Son of God.

6. His special insight into Jesus' power (vv. 50-51)

"Jesus answered, and said unto him, Because I said unto thee, I saw thee under the fig tree, believest thou? [Literally, this is a statement not a question.] Thou shalt see greater things than these. And he saith unto him, Verily, verily, I say unto you, Hereafter ye shall see heaven open, and the angels of God ascending and descending upon the Son of man."

Nathanael witnessed Christ's omniscience and was immediately convinced of who He was because he knew that only God was omniscient. Then Jesus basically said to him, "Nathanael, if you think you saw divine power in that one act of omniscience, you haven't seen anything yet! From here on out you're going to see things going on all the time between heaven and earth. You're going to see heaven open and angels going up and down, and the Son of man working in response to heavenly power."

Nathanael did indeed see heaven and earth linked in Christ as He performed miracle after miracle after miracle. And it may well be that he understood the glory of Christ better than anybody else. It's not recorded that he ever asked another question or framed another query. In fact, he never even appears again, in any detail, in Scripture. He was as solid as a rock from the very start.

So, we meet Nathanael Bartholomew. He was a seeker of truth, prejudiced (but not bound by it), honest, open, a man of prayer, a·man of meditation, a man who made a complete surrender to Christ, and a man with a keen mind and a heart of faith. He saw—and understood. Jesus promised him wonderful revelations of His power, and from then on he saw heaven's power displayed on earth. Philip, however, was never sure what was going on.

God uses slow, plodding, dull, thick, mechanical, analytical, weak, faithless skeptics like Philip. And He also uses people like Nathanael who have great faith, clear understandings, and meditative souls. God can take any raw material available and transform it into what He can use because He's in the business of making the most out of the unqualified.

Do you qualify among the unqualified? If you do, the Lord wants to use you.

Focusing on the Facts

1. What kind of people does God use to advance His kingdom? Give some examples of the people He has used (see pp. 56-57).
2. Why is it significant that Philip is mentioned first in the list of the disciples in the second group (see p. 59)?
3. Where was Philip from? How had he probably established a relationship with Peter and Andrew (John 1:44; see p. 59)?
4. Which disciple did Christ first give a direct call to (John 1:43; see p. 59)?
5. What kind of heart did Philip have? Support your answer (John 1:45; see pp. 59-60).
6. Did Jesus find Philip, or did Philip find Jesus (see p. 60)?
7. What two attributes of Philip are found in John 1:43-46 (see p. 60)?
8. What is one of the most fertile soils for evangelism? Why (see p. 60)?
9. Why did Jesus single Philip out to figure out a way to feed the multitude that had come to Him (John 6:5-6; see p. 61)?
10. How did Philip know that the amount of money they had wouldn't be enough to buy enough food to feed the multitude (John 6:7; see pp. 61-62)?
11. What was the Lord trying to teach Philip by asking him how to feed the multitude (see p. 62)?
12. What level did Philip operate on? What did he have little understanding of (see p. 62)?
13. Why did the Greeks mentioned in John 12:20 approach Philip about seeing Jesus (see p. 63)?
14. What is significant about Philip asking Andrew if the Greeks could see Jesus (see p. 63)?
15. What did Philip not understand about the purpose of Christ (see p. 63)?
16. What was wrong with Philip's spiritual vision and faith (see p. 64)?
17. According to tradition, what happened to Philip (see p. 64)?
18. Describe the difference between Nathanael and Philip (see p. 65).
19. Based on John 1:45, what kind of man was Nathanael (see p. 65)?
20. Define prejudice. How did Nathanael manifest it? How did he overcome it (John 1:46; see pp. 65-66)?
21. Who is a true Jew (Rom. 2:28-29; see p. 66)?
22. Why did Jesus say of Nathanael, "in whom is no guile" (John 1:47; see p. 67)?
23. What was Nathanael possibly doing when he was under a fig tree (John 1:48; see p. 67)?
24. What was Nathanael's response to Jesus' demonstration of omniscience (John 1:49; see pp. 67-68)?
25. What did Jesus promise that Nathanael would see (John 1:50-51; see p. 68)?

Pondering the Principles

1. In what ways are you unqualified to serve God? Since God uses unqualified people, He can use you. In what ways does God need to transform your life so that He can use you? Be specific. You also must be willing to allow God's transforming power free course in your life. Memorize Romans 12:2, "Do not be conformed to this world, but be transformed by the renewing of your mind, that you may prove what the will of God is, that which is good and acceptable and perfect" (NASB).

2. Do you have any unsaved friends? What are you doing to witness to them? There are two ways that you can witness to your unsaved friends: by your words and deeds. What kind of witness are you presenting to your unsaved friends through your words and deeds? What changes do you need to make in your life to be a better witness for Christ? Commit yourself to make those changes.

3. Based on the definition of prejudice found on page 66, do you have a tendency to be prejudiced? Why? Read Ephesians 4:1-6. Are you being diligent to preserve the unity of the Spirit? Based on verse 2, what do you need to do to preserve that unity? Do you presently have an opportunity where God can use you to preserve the unity of the Spirit? Begin to practice the characteristics found in verse 2. Ask God to help you to be sensitive to His leading as you seek to do His will.

5

The Master's Men—Part 3

Outline

Introduction

Review
I. The Initiation of the Apostles
II. The Impact of the Apostles
III. The Identity of the Apostles
    A. Simon Peter
    B. Andrew
    C. James the Son of Zebedee
    D. John
    E. Philip
    F. Bartholomew (Nathanael)

Lesson
    G. Matthew
        1. His recognition of Jesus' forgiveness of sin
        2. His response to Jesus' call
            a) The denunciation of his career
            b) The desire to win others
    H. Thomas
        1. John 11:14-16
            a) The circumstance detailed
            b) The characteristics described
                (1) His initiative
                (2) His pessimism
                (3) His courage
                (4) His faith and love
        2. John 14:5
            a) The circumstance detailed
            b) The characteristics described
        3. John 20:24-29
            a) The circumstance detailed
            b) The characteristics described

Introduction

We have been discussing twelve very special individuals—men who were chosen by our Lord to be His apostles. Their task? To proclaim the gospel of Jesus Christ to the world. It's interesting that the Lord only chose twelve men for such an incredible task—twelve unqualified men at that! Yet, they literally turned the world upside down for Jesus Christ. God can do amazing things against tremendous odds with only a few men. The Old Testament gives us many examples of this.

1. *Elijah* slew 450 false prophets single-handedly (1 Kings 18:40).

2. *Samson* slew 1,000 Philistines with the jawbone of an ass (Judg. 15:15).

3. *Shamgar* slew 600 Philistines with an oxgoad, which was nothing more than a sharpened stick (Judg. 3:31).

4. *Deborah* and *Barak,* along with an army of only 10,000 defeated the massive Canaanite army led by Sisera and his 900 chariots of iron (Judg. 4). According to Josephus, the Jewish historian, Sisera's forces also had 10,000 horsemen and 300,000 footmen.

5. *Gideon,* with an army of only 300 men, defeated a Midianite army of 135,000 (Judg. 7; cf. 8:10).

6. *Jonathan* and his armor bearer faced an overwhelming Philistine army of "thirty thousand chariots, and six thousand horsemen, and people as the sand which is on the seashore in multitude" (1 Sam. 13:5a). In fact, they faced this enemy alone because "when the men of Israel saw that they were hedged in (for the people were distressed), then the people did hide themselves in caves, and thickets, and among rocks, and in high places, and in pits" (13:6). But Jonathan had a little different perspective of the situation as revealed by what he said to his armor bearer: "Come, and let us go over unto the garrison of these uncircumcised: it may be that the Lord will work for us; for there is no restraint to the Lord to save by many or by few" (14:6). Jonathan believed that God could put all of His divine power into one person as easily as He could a multitude of people. Well, Jonathan's faith was rewarded with a victory over a Philistine garrison, slaying about twenty men. According to 14:15, this caused "trembling in the host, in the field, and among all the people; the garrison, and the spoilers, they also trembled, and the earth quaked: so it was a very great trembling." And before every-

thing was over, "all the men of Israel who had hidden themselves in Mount Ephraim, when they heard that the Philistines fled, even they also followed hard after them in the battle. So the Lord saved Israel that day" (vv. 22-23a).

The point is this: God can accomplish His purposes with a multitude of people or just a few—it doesn't matter. As we look at the apostles, we see twelve men who literally turned the world upside down. They established the church, extended the kingdom, and touched the entire world—these twelve, simple, humble men.

Review

In our study of the apostles, we have been examining the question What kind of people does God use? We have discovered that God uses common, unqualified people.

I. THE INITIATION OF THE APOSTLES

II. THE IMPACT OF THE APOSTLES

III. THE IDENTITY OF THE APOSTLES

A. Simon Peter (see pp. 26-36)

The Lord uses strong, bold leaders like Peter, who take charge, initiate, plan, strategize, confront, and command people to Christ, yet make big blunders.

B. Andrew (see pp. 40-44)

God uses humble, gentle, inconspicuous souls like Andrew, who seek no prominence but quietly bring people to Christ.

C. James the Son of Zebedee (see pp. 44-48)

He uses zealous, passionate, uncompromising, task-oriented, insensitive, ambitious men like James.

D. John (see pp. 48-53)

He uses sensitive, tender, loving, people-oriented, believing, intimate truth-seekers like John.

E. Philip (see pp. 58-65)

He uses skeptical, analytical, mechanical, slow-witted, weak-faithed, visionless, pessimistic, insecure men like Philip.

F. Bartholomew (Nathanael; see pp. 65-68)

He also uses truth-seeking, honest, open, clear-minded, meditative, deeply surrendered men like Nathanael Bartholomew, who are full of faith and understanding, and yet are flawed by such a serious sin as prejudice.

Let's look at the two apostles in group two: Matthew and Thomas.

Lesson

G. Matthew

Matthew is mentioned in each of the four lists of apostles, always in the same group. But very little is said about him in the gospels. In fact, the only picture we have of him is given in one incident. This incident is found in Matthew 9:9-13, Mark 2:14-17, and Luke 5:27-32, but we will look at the account in Matthew's gospel.

1. His recognition of Jesus' forgiveness of sin

"And as Jesus passed forth from there, he saw a man, named Matthew, sitting at the tax office; and he saith unto him, Follow me. And he arose, and followed him" (v. 9).

Now, why does Matthew even comment about himself here in verse 9? What's his point? Well, in verses 1-8, Matthew is giving a demonstration that Jesus came to forgive sin. In verses 5-6 Jesus says, "For which is easier, to say, Thy sins be forgiven thee; or to say, Arise, and walk? But that ye may know that the Son of man hath power on earth to forgive sins (then saith he to the sick of the palsy), Arise, take up thy bed, and go unto thine house." Then in verse 9, Matthew slips himself into the account to show that indeed Jesus *can* forgive sin, since He forgave such a vile sinner as himself.

Over in Matthew 10:3, when Matthew puts his name in the list of apostles, he writes, "Matthew, the tax collector." May I hasten to add that no other disciple in the list is associated with his job. Why does Matthew make reference to himself as a tax collector? Was it something to be proud of? No! A tax collector was the most hated, despised, despicable human being in the society of Israel. *Matthew was simply showing us his genuine humility and sense of sinful unworthiness.*

Throughout the narrative of the gospels, Matthew never speaks, never asks a question, never makes a comment, and never appears in any other incident. This is possibly because he was so overwrought by the sin of his life that once he was forgiven he felt unworthy to even speak a word. So, he is the silent man—until the Spirit of God asks him to pick up his pen. Then he is given the privilege of writing the opening of the New Testament—twenty-eight chapters on the majesty of the King of kings Himself.

Matthew: The "Little Mokhes" of Capernaum

Matthew was a traitor, an extortioner, a thief, and an outcast—and he knew it! You see, Matthew was a publican, a Jew hired by the Roman government to collect taxes from his fellow Jews to give to Rome. He was a first-class traitor who worked for the oppressor. And not only that, but he bought the right from the Roman government to collect taxes—so he bought into their system. Now the government would stipulate a certain amount of tax that had to be given to Rome, but then the publican was free to keep anything else he collected. This led to bribes, extortion, and other abuses.

There were two other major classes of tax collectors: the Gabbai and the Mokhes. The Gabbai were the general tax collectors who collected property tax, income tax, and poll tax. These taxes were standardized so there was apparently little graft at this level.

The second class of tax collectors was the Mokhes, and they collected duty on everything. They set up their table where the roads crossed and collected on all the imports and exports, and everything bought and sold. They set tolls on roads, bridges, harbors, axles, donkeys, packages, letters, and so on. They taxed everything they could. Now, there were two kinds of Mokhes: a Great Mokhes and a Little Mokhes. A Great Mokhes hired someone to do the tax collecting for him so he could fade into the background. He really didn't want to be associated with the actual activity itself, and thus retained some of his dignity. A Little Mokhes was too cheap and too greedy to hire somebody to collect the taxes, so he did it himself. He didn't care about the social stigma associated with such a job. This is what Matthew was—a Little Mokhes. In Matthew 9:9 we see him "sitting at the tax office." He was a greedy extortioner and traitor to his people.

2. His response to Jesus' call

   a) The denunciation of his career (v. 9*b*)

      "And he saith unto him, Follow me. And he arose, and followed him."

When Matthew walked away from his tax table, he walked away from his career. A lot more was at stake for him than for the fishermen who left their nets. If following Jesus didn't work out for them, they could always go back to fishing—their nets and boats would still be there. In fact, in John 21 they did go back to fishing—but only until the Lord came and straightened them out. However, when Matthew walked away from his tax table, I'm sure the Roman government had somebody else there the next day—cutting off his career for good.

b) The desire to win others (vv. 10-13)

"And it came to pass, as Jesus sat eating in the house, behold, many tax collectors and sinners came and sat down with him and his disciples. (According to Luke 5:29, this was a feast that Matthew had prepared in his own house.) And when the Pharisees saw it, they said unto his disciples, Why eateth your Master with tax collectors and sinners? But when Jesus heard that, he said unto them, They that are well need not a physician, but they that are sick. But go and learn what that meaneth, I will have mercy, and not sacrifice; for I am not come to call the righteous, but sinners to repentance."

The point of Matthew's banquet was for Jesus to call sinners to repentance. He had a heart for the lost. There are some people in this world who just gravitate to the down-and-outers, and Matthew was one of them. He was ready to share the poverty of his Master, but he first used his riches to introduce sinners to Christ.

I'm glad that when the Lord put together a team of twelve men, He took some of them from out of the deepest pit of sin. Why? So that we would see the possibilities of reaching people in that pit for Christ, and their potential once they are saved.

I believe the whole thread running through the first part of Matthew 9 is confession of sin, repentance, and forgiveness. The reason Matthew inserts his conversion experience where he does is because of his deep sense of sin and forgiveness. He knew his sin, his graft, his abuse, his extortion, his greed, and his betrayal of his people. He knew what he was, and I believe he despised it and wanted out. I believe that he had heard Jesus preach in that little town of Capernaum and knew that when Jesus said to him, "Follow me," inherent in that was the forgiveness of his sin. So, he was willing to say good-bye to his career and everything else because he wanted forgiveness.

What kind of people does God use? Stained glass saints? No. Vile, wretched, rotten sinners. He uses the most despicable people in society—as long as they repent from their sins and are willing to be forgiven through faith in Jesus Christ. You say, "Well, God can't do much with people who have that kind of evil past." Oh, really? God used Matthew to write the first gospel of the New Testament. You see, God is in the restoration business. He takes the unqualified and transforms them. Sure, he was a criminal—an outcast—the most hated of men, but he was so utterly convinced of his sin that when he was given an opportunity to believe, he immediately did so. He became a man of quiet humility who loved the outcasts and gave no place to the religious establishment—a man of great faith and total, utter surrender to the lordship of Jesus Christ.

That brings us to the last man in group two.

H. Thomas

What is the first word you think of when you think of Thomas? Probably *doubt.* This is unfortunate because I believe Thomas has gotten bad press—he's a better man than you think. Most people see Thomas as a doubter, but I'm going to show you some things about Thomas that may change your opinion of him.

Of the four gospels, only John opens Thomas up to us. Let's look at these three brief texts so that we can get to know the real Thomas.

1. John 11:14-16

   a) The circumstance detailed

   As we approach chapter 11, Jesus and His disciples had left Jerusalem because the plot to take His life had become more pronounced (John 10:39) and it wasn't His time to die. As they were staying by the Jordan River where John the Baptist had first done his baptizing, Jesus received the news that His beloved and close friend Lazarus was sick. But instead of immediately going to Lazarus to make him well, as his sisters Mary and Martha had wanted Him to do, He waited for two days (11:6). Why? Because He wanted to give Lazarus sufficient time to die. You say, "Why did Jesus want Lazarus to die?" Look at verses 14-15: "Then said Jesus unto them plainly, Lazarus is dead. And I am glad for your sakes that I was not there, to the intent ye may believe; nevertheless, let us go unto him." In other words, Jesus let him die so that He could increase their faith by performing a miracle and displaying His power.

When Jesus said, "let us go unto him," the disciples panicked. Why? Because Lazarus's body was in Bethany—and Bethany was only two miles east of Jerusalem. Now that was a scary announcement, and I am sure they must have thought, "This is suicide. We can't go back there!" (cf. 11:8). And possibly, some of the disciples were even getting ready to leave Him. It's at this point that Thomas enters the scene and says, "Let us also go, that we may die with him" (v. 16b).

b) The characteristics described

Several characteristics stand out as we look at Thomas in this circumstance.

(1) His initiative

I see a certain amount of initiative and leadership as Thomas kind of takes over, rises to the top, and says, "Wait a minute, guys! Let's go with Him and die with Him."

(2) His pessimism

I also see pessimism in his statement. He was convinced that if Jesus went near Jerusalem He would be killed, along with all those who went with Him. It was all very clear to Thomas—he was sure of it!

(3) His courage

The greatest courage in the world is not the courage of an optimist, because an optimist always expects the best. I believe that the greatest courage in the world is the courage of a pessimist because he expects the worst and is still willing to follow through. Thomas could see nothing but disaster ahead—in fact, he probably had figured out his epitaph—yet he was determined to go with Christ and die with Him.

(4) His faith and love

Why was Thomas so willing to die with Jesus? It certainly wasn't because he doubted Him. Rather, it was because he so totally believed Him. And along with this faith, I believe he had such a deep, intense love for Jesus, perhaps only equaled by John, that he could not endure existence without Him. In other words, he's saying, "If Jesus is going to die, then let's go die with Him. The alternative is to be without Him." These are the words of love and faith—wanting to be wherever Jesus was even to the point of dying and still being with Him. This was a man with deep love for Jesus.

2. John 14:5

   a) The circumstance detailed

   In John 14:1-4, Jesus gives the following announcement to His disciples, "Let not your heart be troubled; ye believe in God, believe also in me. In my Father's house are many mansions (lit., 'rooms'); if it were not so, I would have told you. I go to prepare a place for you. And if I go and prepare a place for you, I will come again, and receive you unto myself, that where I am, there ye may be also. And where I go ye know, and the way ye know." Then in verse 5, Thomas speaks up and says, "Lord, we know not where thou goest; and how can we know the way?"

   b) The characteristics described

   The statement that Thomas makes in verse 5 is spoken from the same heart that said, "Lord, don't go somewhere we can't go" back in John 11. The issue with Thomas was the thought of being separated from Jesus. In other words, Thomas was saying, "Lord, I don't like what I hear. You say that You're going to leave us, and that we know where You're going and how to get there—but we *don't* know and we'll *never* find the place." Remember, Thomas is a pessimist, and I believe he is speaking from a broken, bewildered, bleak, negative heart.

   In verse 6 Jesus answers Thomas's question: "I am the way, the truth, and the life; no man cometh unto the Father, but by me." What He's saying is, "Thomas, I'll take you there. I'm the way, so you don't have to fear." Again we see Thomas's pessimism as well as his intense love for Jesus.

3. John 20:24-29

   a) The circumstance detailed

   Jesus is crucified in John 19, and when He dies, Thomas is shattered. He probably said, "I knew it would happen!

He died, and I didn't die with Him. He went away, and I don't know where He is." All of his fears had come true and he felt betrayed, rejected, and forsaken. Like a wounded animal, he retreated to be alone and to lick his wounds. So when all the rest of the disciples came together, he wasn't there. Thomas was extremely depressed because he loved so deeply. He would have died with Jesus—but Jesus died without Him. He wanted to go with Jesus—but Jesus went without him. His pessimism was vindicated, and he was in the pit of despair.

In John 20:24-25 we read, "But Thomas, one of the twelve, called Didymus, was not with them when Jesus came. The other disciples, therefore, said unto him, We have seen the Lord. But he said unto them, Except I shall see in his hands the print of the nails, and put my finger into the print of the nails, and thrust my hand into his side, I will not believe." Did you ever try to talk to somebody who is depressed? It's difficult, isn't it? Thomas was depressed, and remember, he's also a pessimist. He was basically saying, "I've got to see it to believe it."

Before you pounce on Thomas and label him as "the doubter," kindly remember that *none* of the disciples believed that Jesus had risen until *they* saw Him. After all, it's not easy to believe that somebody rose from the dead. So don't make Thomas the doubter; he was a loving pessimist.

By the way, the Lord doesn't mind it when people want to be sure. In the case of Thomas, He accommodated his desire to see Him firsthand. Look at verses 26-29: "And, after eight days, again his disciples were inside, and Thomas was with them; then came Jesus, the doors being shut, and stood in the midst, and said, Peace be unto you. [That was certainly a fitting greeting after walking through a wall.] Then saith he to Thomas [zeroing in on this dear soul who was utterly depressed and shattered], Reach here thy finger, and behold my hands; and reach here thy hand, and thrust it into my side; and be not faithless, but believing." It doesn't say that Thomas did any of that, he just immediately answered Jesus and said, "My Lord and my God." In this greatest single confession ever made, Thomas affirmed the deity and the lordship of Jesus Christ. Then in verse 29 Jesus says, "Thomas, because thou hast seen me, thou hast believed; blessed are they that have not seen, and yet have believed."

b) The characteristics described

Thomas was melancholy, moody, pessimistic, comfortless, and shattered, but when he saw the Lord Jesus Christ, he gave the greatest testimony ever given. In fact, that one little statement literally destroys the lie that Jesus is not God! All the "isms," schisms, and spasms that come along and deny the deity of Christ are utterly put to silence by Thomas.

From this account in John 20, two practical truths seem to stand out: (1) Jesus doesn't blame someone for wanting to be sure; (2) surety comes most likely in the fellowship of other believers. Thomas missed out the first time Jesus appeared to the disciples because he wasn't there. Now, that doesn't mean that a person can't find Christ in solitude, but that it's more likely to occur among the fellowship of those who believe.

One tradition tells us that Thomas was killed when, because of his faith, a spear was rammed through his body. It was a fitting climax for one who was told to reach forth his hand and feel the spear mark in his own Lord.

What kind of people does God use? Vile sinners like Matthew, and tender-hearted, moody, melancholy pessimists like Thomas. All the apostles were unique individuals and our Lord used them to change the world. If you are available He can use you too. Remember, His purposes *will* be accomplished—by many or by few.

Focusing on the Facts

1. Give some examples of people that God used to do His will against seemingly impossible odds (see pp. 72-73).
2. What did Jonathan believe about God's divine power (1 Sam. 14:6; see p. 72)?
3. Why does Matthew include an account involving himself in his gospel (Matt. 9:9-13; see p. 74)?
4. What had been Matthew's occupation before he became a disciple? What was his purpose in revealing that fact (Matt. 10:3; see p. 74)?
5. What was a publican? What was his job (see p. 75)?
6. Describe the two kinds of tax collectors and their duties. What kind was Matthew (see p. 75)?
7. What did Matthew give up when he followed Jesus (Matt. 9:9; see p. 76)?
8. Why did Matthew hold a banquet and invite Jesus (Matt. 9:10-13; see p. 76)?

9. Although God can use the most despicable people, what must they do before that can happen (see p. 77)?
10. Why did Jesus wait for Lazarus to die before going to Bethany, instead of rushing to heal him (John 11:14-15; see pp. 77-78)?
11. What characteristics did Thomas reveal when he encouraged the rest of the disciples to follow Jesus to Bethany? Explain each one (John 11:16; see pp. 78-79).
12. What kind of person truly has great courage (see p. 78)?
13. Why was Thomas so willing to die with Jesus (see pp. 78-79)?
14. Explain what Thomas meant when he said, "Lord, we know not where thou goest; and how can we know the way?" (John 14:5; see p. 79).
15. What lie did Thomas's confession in John 20:28 destroy (see p. 80)?
16. What two practical truths stand out in John 20:24-29 (see p. 81)?

Pondering the Principles

1. God has accomplished tremendous things with a few men against impossible odds. He can also accomplish great things in your life despite seemingly impossible odds. Read Mark 9:17-27. Did the man believe that Jesus could help his son? What does Jesus say in verse 23? How did the man respond? Have you faced any situation that you never thought the Lord could handle? Based on this study, how would you respond if you faced a similar situation? Memorize Mark 9:23: "All things are possible to him who believes." Apply that verse whenever you face a seemingly impossible situation.
2. Several characteristics stood out in Thomas's life: initiative, courage, faith, and love. In what ways are you manifesting those characteristics in your life? Be specific. In what ways do you need to improve in those areas? Is your commitment to Christ as great as Thomas's was? Take this time to reaffirm your commitment to Christ. Prayerfully consider how you might serve Him better.

6

The Master's Men—Part 4

Outline

Introduction

Review
I. The Initiation of the Apostles
II. The Impact of the Apostles
III. The Identity of the Apostles
    A. Simon Peter
    B. Andrew
    C. James the Son of Zebedee
    D. John
    E. Philip
    F. Bartholomew (Nathanael)
    G. Matthew
    H. Thomas

Lesson
I. James the Son of Alphaeus
    1. His inferred characteristics
        a) His stature
        b) His age
        c) His influence
    2. His invisibility
    3. His implied family
        a) His brother
        b) His cousin
    J. Lebbaeus (Surnamed Thaddaeus)
    1. The significance of his appellations
        a) His given name
        b) His nicknames
            (1) Thaddaeus
            (2) Lebbaeus
    2. The specifics of his appearance
        a) The comment
        b) The confusion

Introduction

Henry Drummond, an author and preacher, was once invited to speak at a very elite, high-class West End club in London. Upon his arrival, he found that all of the club members were assembled and everything was arranged for his message. He began his speech with this very provocative truth: "Ladies and gentlemen, the entrance fee into the Kingdom of heaven is nothing, but the annual subscription is everything." It was a well-stated introduction.

In this series from Matthew 10, we have been examining men who were willing to give everything and go to the ultimate sacrifice. They were willing to turn their backs on their professions, their lifestyles, their homes, and their own choices in life, to follow Jesus Christ. They walked away from their nets, their tax tables, their political involvements, and their enterprises. Why? Because they were totally committed to following Jesus Christ wherever He led them. And may I add that the twelve were the few among the many who were *not* so willing to be committed.

Jesus had many followers. Unnumbered multitudes followed Him because they were attracted to His personal magnetism, the power and truth in what He said, and His ability to do miracles, signs, and wonders. This mass of people who followed Jesus could be classified as disciples, because the Greek word for disciple, *mathētēs,* simply means "a learner." These people were learning about Him, but the word *disciple* doesn't say anything about commitment. That is why Matthew 10 starts out with twelve disciples and then one verse later calls them "apostles." First they were "learners," then they were "sent ones"—when they showed that they had learned their lessons.

There were many disciples who were not willing to make a total commitment. Luke 9:57-62 gives us an account of some disciples who wanted to follow Jesus, but one of them wanted to first bury his father, another wanted to say good-bye to his relatives, and still another wanted comfort. In contrast to the twelve, those disciples weren't willing to pay the price of commitment.

Now, why am I saying all this? Because I'm about to introduce you to three apostles whom we know very little about. But at least we can know with certainty that they were totally committed to Christ. Sometimes when the obscure names of James the son of Alphaeus, Lebbaeus (surnamed Thaddaeus), and Simon the Zealot are looked at, the tendency is to see them as a second-class or out-of-the-way stragglers. But the fact of the matter is that they made the same commitment that the other apostles made—they too crossed over the line in total obedience to Christ.

Something worthless made valuable

Throughout this series we've been looking at the question What kind of people does God use? And we've seen that the Lord uses all kinds. In fact, we've seen that the Lord can take any kind of raw material and use it for the advancement of His glorious, eternal kingdom. This principle can be illustrated by the following:

Longfellow could take a worthless piece of paper, write a poem on it, and instantly make it worth thousands of dollars—and it's called genius.

Rockefeller could sign his name to a piece of paper and make it worth millions of dollars—and it's called riches.

A mechanic can take material worth only five dollars and make it worth five hundred—and it's called skill.

An artist can make a fifty-cent piece of canvas, paint a picture on it, and make it worth thousands of dollars—and it's called art.

Jesus Christ can take a worthless, sinful life, wash it in His blood, put His Spirit in it, and make it valuable to God—and that's called sanctification.

The Lord is in the business of taking rough, raw material and using it—transforming men by His power to be the extension of His work in the world.

The Hands of Christ

During the Second World War, a church in Strasbourg was destroyed. After the bombing, the members of this particular church went to see what was left and found that the entire roof had fallen in, leaving a heap of rubble and broken glass. Much to their surprise, however, a statue of Christ with outstretched hands that had been carved centuries before by a great artist was still standing erect. It was virtually unharmed except that both hands had been sheared off by a falling beam. The people hurried to a sculptor in town and asked if he could replace the

> hands of the statue. He was willing, and he even offered to do it for nothing. The church officials met to consider the sculptor's proposition—and decided not to accept his offer. Why? Because they felt that the statue without the hands would be the greatest illustration possible that God's work is done through His people.
>
> In a very real sense that's true. Jesus Christ chooses human hands. Sometimes they seem to be the most infirm hands, the least potentially successful hands, or the least qualified hands—but those are the hands He uses.

The Bible doesn't really say anything about James the son of Alphaeus, Lebbaeus (surnamed Thaddaeus), or Simon the Zealot—the first three apostles of group three. But one thing we do know—they were chosen by Christ to be His apostles, and as such, taught the truths of the kingdom, healed the sick, and cast out demons. They were the first order of kingdom preachers after Christ Himself, and will reign on thrones ruling the twelve tribes of Israel in the Millennium.

Review

I. THE INITIATION OF THE APOSTLES

II. THE IMPACT OF THE APOSTLES

III. THE IDENTITY OF THE APOSTLES

A. Simon Peter (see pp. 26-36)

B. Andrew (see pp. 40-44)

C. James the Son of Zebedee (see pp. 44-48)

D. John (see pp. 48-53)

E. Philip (see pp. 58-65)

F. Bartholomew (Nathanael) (see pp. 65-68)

G. Matthew (see pp. 74-77)

H. Thomas (see pp. 77-81)

Lesson

Let's continue our study of the apostles with a look at the first man in group three.

I. James the Son of Alphaeus

The only thing the Bible tells us about James the son of Alphaeus is his name. That's it! It's not known if he ever wrote anything, and nothing he ever said, asked, or did is recorded in the Bible.

1. His inferred characteristics

   In Mark 15:40 he is called "James the less." The Greek word used in this title is *mikros,* which means "little." In other words, he was "little James." From this reference we can make some references as to:

   a) His stature

   The word *mikros* basically means "small in stature." So it's possible that he was little. If he was large, they probably woudn't have called him "little James."

   b) His age

   Mikros can also mean "young in age." If he had been older than James the son of Zebedee, they probably wouldn't have called him *mikros,* because it would have been confusing. If anything, they would have called him "James the elder," or "older James." So, it probably indicates that he was younger.

   c) His influence

   "Little James" could also have had reference to his having little influence. If he had been a very influential man, he probably would have been nicknamed "bold James" or something like that, but not "little James."

   So, it may well be that James was just a small young guy with a personality that was not particularly powerful. It's encouraging to know that the Lord doesn't depend upon superstars, isn't it?

2. His invisibility

   James the son of Alphaeus will sit on a throne, reigning over one of the tribes of Israel in the Millennium—and what do we know about him? Nothing! His distinguishing mark is obscurity. He sought no recognition, displayed no great leadership, asked no critical questions, demonstrated no unusual insight. It just may be that he was so obedient that there wasn't a lot to say about him. Peter appears all the time—but it's usually negative. It's possible that he went where he was sent by Jesus, fought the good fight, finished his course, and kept the faith without any need for applause or notice. Only his name remains—his labors are sunk in obscurity.

   The Lord uses ordinary people to do extraordinary things—silent, unknown soldiers. James the son of Alphaeus reminds me of the nameless people mentioned in Hebrews 11:33-38 "who, through faith, subdued kingdoms, wrought righteousness, obtained promises, stopped the mouths of lions, quenched the violence of fire, escaped the edge of the sword, out of weakness were made strong, became valiant in fight, turned to flight the armies of the aliens. Women received their dead raised to life again, and others were tortured, not accepting deliverance, that they might obtain a better resurrection: And others had trial of cruel mockings and scourgings, yea, moreover, of bonds and imprisonment; they were stoned, they were sawn asunder, were tested, were slain with the sword; they wandered about in sheepskins and goatskins; being destitute, afflicted, tormented." The writer of Hebrews mentions all these nameless people who died for their faith, and then he adds, "Of whom the world was not worthy." The world wasn't worthy of these silent, unknown soldiers of faith.

3. His implied family

   a) His brother

   Both James and Alphaeus are common names. But another disciple also had a father named Alphaeus—Matthew. According to Mark 2:14, Levi (or Matthew) is referred to as "the son of Alphaeus." So there's a remote possibility that James and Matthew were brothers.

   b) His cousin

   In John 19:25, when our Lord was dying on the cross, it says, "Now there stood by the cross of Jesus His mother, and His mother's sister, Mary, the wife of Clopas." We can assume that no mother would name two of her daughters Mary, so Mary the wife of Clopas was the sister-in-law of Mary the mother of Jesus. Since Clopas is another form of the name Alphaeus, it's possible that Alphaeus was Joseph's brother. If that was the case, Jesus and James were cousins.

   Further, this idea is substantiated by the fact that Mark 15:40 refers to Mary as "the mother of James the less."

   So it's possible that James was the brother of Matthew, or the cousin of Jesus—or even both. Now if it is true that he was Jesus' cousin, he might have tried to throw his weight around a little—but we don't see him doing that. He just remains obscure.

The instrument is immaterial

The apostles demonstrate to us that the emphasis in kingdom work is never on the worker. This is seen by the fact that the

New Testament never focuses on them. It doesn't say, "Now, it's very important to study these twelve men. You must study their career, their style, their method, and their means." The Bible doesn't pick out the best preacher and give his homiletic method, or the best healer and give his technique, or anybody who's the most effective at anything—it doesn't even deal with them. The only time the apostles are even mentioned is when they intersect with Christ for a specific purpose. *He* is the focus. The human instrument is immaterial to God. He can use Balaam's ass if He has to (Num. 22:28-30) or even make the rocks cry out (Luke 19:40). *The human instrument is never the issue because the focus is always on Jesus Christ.*

An illustration of this is the great artist who painted a picture of the Last Supper. When he finished, he called in his friend to look at it and give his evaluation. After gazing at it for some time the friend remarked, "Those cups that are on the table are the most magnificent cups I've ever seen!" To the astonishment of the dumbfounded friend, the artist immediately picked up his brush and some paint and painted over each cup, saying, "I failed. I wanted you to see Christ—but you saw cups."

It's a wonderful thing to be a vessel fit for the Master's use, but that's not where the focus is to be. *One of the great tragedies of modern Christianity is that we focus on the cups and don't see Christ.* We are personality oriented, studying the method and means of men rather than experiencing the power of God. And I believe this "Christian superstar" mentality is part of the reason for the impotence in the church. Christ is to be the focus—not men.

So the Lord used an obscure, little, unknown, unsung man. He may have been able to claim that he was Matthew's brother or even Jesus' cousin, but he went quietly unnoticed through the entire gospel narrative. Someday, we'll be able to read the heavenly record for ourselves and find out all about him.

Let's look at the second apostle mentioned in group three.

J. Lebbaeus (Surnamed Thaddaeus)

1. The significance of his appellations

   a) His given name

      In Matthew 10:3 one of the apostles is identified as "Lebbaeus, whose surname was Thaddaeus." This same apostle is also referred to in Luke 6:16 and Acts 1:13 as "Judas the son of James" (NASB). And in John 14:21 he's called "Judas (not Iscariot)" (NASB). Judas was probably the name given to him at birth. It was a common Hebrew name which meant "Jehovah leads."

b) His nicknames

I believe that the names Lebbaeus and Thaddaeus were added at a later time to reflect his character—like nicknames. As such, an understanding of the meaning of these names will give us insight into some of his possible attributes.

(1) Thaddaeus

The name Thaddaeus comes from the Hebrew root *thad,* which has to do with the female breast. Basically, Thaddaeus means "breast-child." Perhaps this name was given to him by his parents because he was the youngest child—the "baby" of the family—or because he was especially cherished by his mother. So, his family nickname was probably Thaddaeus.

(2) Lebbaeus

The name Lebbaeus comes from the Hebrew root *leb,* which means "heart." Literally, the name means "heart-child" and it usually referred to someone who was courageous.

We can't be sure, but it's possible that his family saw him as their baby and his friends saw him as a man of hard courage.

2. The specifics of his appearance

Judas Lebbaeus Thaddaeus was a man wrapped in obscurity, but he did ask one very important question—the only time we meet him in Scripture. Let's look at John 14:21-24.

a) The comment (v. 21)

Jesus, speaking the night before His trial, says, "He that hath my commandments, and keepeth them, he it is that loveth me; and he that loveth me shall be loved of my Father, and I will love him, and will manifest myself to him."

In this incredibly important statement, Jesus basically says, "I can tell who loves Me by the way they obey Me, and only those who truly love and obey Me will I manifest Myself to." In other words, if someone claims to love God but doesn't obey Him, that claim is a lie and He will not manifest Himself to him. In fact, when people don't know God or perceive His truth, it's because they don't love Him. First there has to be a love toward God and a willingness to obey Him, and then He will manifest Himself. God only manifests Himself to a loving heart.

b) The confusion (v. 22)

The word "manifest" triggered Judas Lebbaeus Thaddaeus to respond to Jesus' comment. "Judas saith unto him, not Iscariot, Lord, how is it that thou wilt manifest thyself unto us, and not unto the world?" Why did he ask this question?

(1) His view of the kingdom

Thaddaeus was thinking of Jesus' manifestation as an outward one. He had followed Jesus with great expectation and hope that He would set up the earthly kingdom and establish Himself as Lord and Savior. So with this idea in mind he asked, "If You don't manifest Yourself to the world, how can You possibly fulfill the messianic hope, set up the kingdom on earth, and reign on the throne of David? How could You possibly demonstrate who You are and the world not see it?"

(2) His humility

His question may also reflect humility, as he asked, "Why would You manifest Yourself only to us and not the whole world? Why would You limit Yourself to this motley group of nobodies. If You're the Messiah and this is the moment, why would You only show Yourself to us? If the Messiah is going to rule the world, why won't everybody see You?"

(3) His courage

Perhaps some of the courage he was known for is also seen in his question. He might have been saying, "If it's time for the kingdom, let's go for it! Show Your power to the whole world and let's get on with it, Lord!"

c) The clarification (vv. 23-24)

Thaddaeus didn't understand what the Lord was saying, so Jesus repeated the same principle again. "Jesus answered, and said unto him, If a man love me, he will keep my words; and my Father will love him, and we will come unto him, and make our abode with him. He that loveth me not keepeth not my sayings; and the word which ye hear is not mine, but the Father's, who sent me."

Basically the Lord said, "Judas Lebbaeus Thaddaeus, the point I'm making is this: The only people who will be able to perceive Me are the ones who love Me. The ones who don't love Me don't know what I'm talking about or where My words come from." In other words, *manifestation is limited to reception.* It's like a radio station. Someone can send the signal out, but until you turn the radio on you can't receive the program.

Robert Louis Stevenson once quoted Thoreau as saying, "It takes two to speak the truth; one to speak and another to hear." John 1:10-11 says, "He was in the world, and the world was made by him, and the world knew him not. He came unto his own, and his own received him not." Why didn't they receive Him? Because "the god of this world hath blinded the minds of them who believe not" (2 Cor. 4:4*a*) and because "men loved darkness rather than light" (John 3:19*b*).

So, Jesus said to Thaddaeus, "I can only manifest Myself to people whose receivers are on. Only those whose hearts are purified by love, and walk in obedience, will know the manifestation of God."

Early church tradition tells us that Thaddaeus was tremendously gifted with the power of God to heal the sick. It is said that a certain king in Syria by the name of Adgar was very ill. When he heard about Thaddaeus's power to heal, he called for Thaddaeus to come and heal him. On his way to the king, says the legend, he healed hundreds of people throughout Syria. When he finally reached King Adgar he healed him and presented the gospel, and the king became a Christian. As a result, however, the country was thrown into such a chaos that an apostate nephew of the king took Thaddaeus prisoner and martyred him. Thaddaeus's symbol, in old church history books, is a big club, because tradition says he was beaten to death with a club. If any part of this legend is true, it again reveals his courage—faithful to his Lord.

K. Simon the Zealot

1. His proper title

In Matthew 10:4 Simon is identified as "Simon, the Canaanite." This is an unfortunate transliteration of the Greek word *Kananaios* assuming that it refers to the geographical location of Canaan. Actually, the word comes from the Hebrew root *qanna,* which means "to be jealous" and was used for those who were jealous for the law. In Luke 6:15 Simon is identified as, "Simon, called Zelotes." The Greek word used here is *zēlōtēs* and has the same meaning as the Hebrew root just mentioned.

The title "Simon the Zealot" may mean that he was actually identified with a party in Judaism known as the Zealots. After becoming a follower of Christ, he must have continued to manifest the same kind of fiery, passionate zeal that he had when he was a Zealot, thus retaining the title.

2. His political background

Let's look at a brief history of the group that Simon was identified with before he became a follower of Christ—the Zealots.

There were basically four dominant groups within Judaism: the Pharisees, Sadducees, Essenes, and Zealots. The Zealots were the last of the great Jewish parties to emerge, and their members were the most fervent, passionate patriots of Judaism. Their existence seems to have come from the Maccabean period when the Jews were led by Judas Maccabaeus in a revolt against Greek influences on their nation and religion. A statement revealing the intensity of this revolutionary philosophy is seen in 1 Maccabees 2:50: "Be ye zealous for the law and give your lives for the covenant." This politically oriented group later became known as the Zealots.

In New Testament times, these red-hot patriots banded together under the leadership of Judas the Galilean to deliver Judea from Roman domination. They murdered, plundered, burned, looted, and were involved in any type of terrorist guerrilla activity that they could inflict. The Romans finally murdered Judas, but they could not stamp out the Zealots' fire. Finally, in A.D. 70 the Romans had to put a stop to all the havoc the Zealots were causing, so they destroyed Jerusalem and slaughtered people in 985 towns in Galilee where the Zealots' attacks were the fiercest.

After the destruction of Jerusalem in A.D. 70, the Zealots came under the leadership of a man by the name of Eleazar. There were only a few Zealots left, but they continued their guerrilla-type activities against the Romans. These activities were enhanced because of a retreat that they had discovered—a place called Masada. Finally, however, the Romans captured Masada. The Zealots, not wanting their lives to be taken by the despised and hated Roman enemy, committed suicide. Josephus, the Jewish historian, in *The Wars of the Jews* (Book VII, Chapters VIII and IX), records an account of this mass suicide. Eleazar summoned the people together and made a flaming speech in which he urged all the men to slaughter their own wives and children and then commit suicide. They took him at his word, tenderly embraced their wives, kissed their children, and began their bloody work. Nine hundred and sixty people perished; two women and five children escaped by hidiing in a cave. The Zealots' hatred of the Romans was so deep that they killed themselves before they would let the Romans take their lives.

Now Simon, to attach himself to this group, must have been a man with a tremendous passion and capacity for zeal. And he must have been a fireball when it came to doing the work of the Lord, because he had found a better leader and a greater cause.

3. His partner in ministry

Notice that Simon is listed right before Judas Iscariot in Matthew 10. I believe that when Jesus sent the apostles out to minister two-by-two (Mark 6:7), Simon and Judas Iscariot went together. They both may have originally followed Christ for the same political reasons, seeing Him as an aid to their political cause. But Simon believed and was transformed—Judas did not.

Note: Think how wonderful it must have been for Simon to get along with Matthew. Matthew collected taxes for the Roman government, and the Zealots were so anti-Roman that they wouldn't even think twice about murdering a Jew who was in any way connected with Rome. It's tremendous to see how this publican and Zealot were able to join hands in the love of Christ.

The music of the Master

There once was a great concert violinist who wanted to demonstrate a very important point, so he rented a music hall and announced that he would play a concert on a $20,000 violin. On the night of the concert the place was packed with violin lovers, curious to hear such an expensive instrument played. The violinist came out on stage and gave an exquisite performance. When he was done, he bowed and took their applause, but suddenly, he threw the violin to the ground, stomped it to pieces, and walked off the stage. The people were horrified. The stage manager then came out and said, "Ladies and gentlemen, to put you at ease, the violin that was just destroyed was only a $20 violin. He will now return to play on the $20,000 instrument." He did so, and few people could tell the difference. The point that he wanted to make was well illustrated, and the point was this: It isn't the violin that makes the music, it's the violinist.

Most of us are $20 violins at best, but in the Master's hands we can make beautiful music. The Lord uses all kinds of unqualified people, doesn't He? And he can use you and me.

Focusing on the Facts

1. What did the twelve give up to follow Jesus? Why did they give up those things (see p. 84)?
2. What did the disciples in Luke 9:57-62 lack (see p. 84)?
3. What can we know for certain about James the son of Alphaeus, Lebbaeus, and Simon the Zealot (see p. 85)?
4. What is it called when Jesus Christ takes a worthless, sinful life, washes it in His blood, puts His Spirit in it, and makes it valuable to God (see p. 85)?
5. What does the Bible say about James the son of Alphaeus (see p. 86)?
6. Based on Mark 15:40, what can be inferred about James the son of Alphaeus (see p. 87)?
7. What is the distinguishing mark of James the son of Alphaeus? Explain (see p. 87).
8. Describe some of James's possible family relationships (see p. 88).
9. Why should the human instrument that God uses never be the issue (see p. 89)?
10. What was Lebbaeus, whose surname was Thaddaeus, also called (Acts 1:13; see pp. 89-90)?
11. Why did he receive the names Lebbaeus and Thaddaeus? What do those names mean (see p. 90)?
12. How is Jesus able to determine those who truly love Him? To whom does Jesus manifest Himself (John 14:21; see pp. 90-91)?
13. What did Lebbaeus ask Jesus in John 14:22? Why? Explain (see pp. 91-92).
14. What was Christ's manifestation of Himself limited to? Explain (see p. 92).
15. Why didn't the men of the world receive Christ (2 Cor. 4:4; see p. 92)?
16. What is one possible explanation for the title "Simon the Zealot" (see p. 93)?
17. Describe the party known as Zealots (see pp. 93-94).
18. What kind of man could Simon have been to be attached to the Zealots (see p. 94)?

Pondering the Principles

1. If you are a Christian, then you had to give up some things to follow Jesus. What did you give up? Be specific. Name some areas of your life that you still need to give up as you follow Christ. Are you anxious to give them up, or do you still hold them as more important than Christ? Read Luke 9:57-62. What were those men unwilling to give up? Read Luke 9:23-25. What does Jesus say is necessary to be His disciple? Are you willing to make that commitment? If so, then begin to follow Christ today.

2. In your service for Christ, do you sometimes hope that others will take notice of your labors? What is wrong with that kind of attitude? Read Philippians 2:3-5. What attitude should you have? Instead of hoping that others will take notice of you, what should you do for them? Make the commitment to fulfill Philippians 2:3-4. Memorize James 4:6: "God is opposed to the proud, but gives grace to the humble" (NASB).

3. It is amazing to realize that two men from such diverse backgrounds and political affiliations as Matthew and Simon the Zealot could be made one in Christ. Think about those Christians that you know and love. How many come from totally different backgrounds than yours? How many believers do you have trouble getting along with? Why do you have trouble? Since all believers are one in Christ, you should be able to get along with every brother and sister. Ask God to reveal to you those deep things in your heart that might be causing you to have the wrong attitude toward a fellow believer. Confess that to God and strive to love all your fellow brothers and sisters in Christ.

7

The Master's Men—Part 5

Outline

Review
I. The Initiation of the Apostles
II. The Impact of the Apostles
III. The Identity of the Apostles
   A. Simon Peter
   B. Andrew
   C. James the Son of Zebedee
   D. John
   E. Philip
   F. Bartholomew (Nathanael)
   G. Matthew
   H. Thomas
   I. James the Son of Alphaeus
   J. Lebbaeus (Surnamed Thaddaeus)
   K. Simon the Zealot

Lesson
   L. Judas Iscariot
      1. His name
         a) Judas
         b) Iscariot
      2. His call
         a) Judas's commitment
         b) Jesus' choice
            (1) Psalm 41:9
            (2) Psalm 55:12-14, 20*b*-21
            (3) Zechariah 11:12-13
         c) Judas's character
         d) Judas's chance
      3. His progress
         a) The setting
            (1) His desire
            (2) His disillusionment

    b) The sequence
        (1) His hatred unmasked
        (2) His hypocrisy exposed
4. His betrayal
    a) Established
        (1) A private place
        (2) A pitiful price
        (3) A personal perversion
    b) Executed
5. His death
6. The lessons learned
    a) Judas is the world's greatest example of lost opportunity
    b) Judas is the world's greatest example of wasted privilege
    c) Judas is the world's greatest illustration of the love of money being the root of evil
    d) Judas is the world's greatest lesson of the forbearing, patient love of God
    e) Judas provided an essential qualification in preparing Christ for His role as our High Priest

Review

We have been studying the Master's men and have tried to learn all we can about them. As we have examined the first eleven apostles, we have attempted to see how their personalities and characteristics fit into the Lord's plan. Up to this point, we have looked at:

I. THE INITIATION OF THE APOSTLES

II. THE IMPACT OF THE APOSTLES

III. THE IDENTITY OF THE APOSTLES

H. Thomas (see pp. 77-81)

I. James the Son of Alphaeus (see pp. 86-89)

J. Lebbaeus (Surnamed Thaddaeus; see pp. 89-92)

K. Simon the Zealot (see pp. 92-95)

Lesson

The last apostle stands out against the background of the others. He is isolated, lonely, and alone. His name?

L. Judas Iscariot

Judas was a horrifying, colossal misfit—the epitome of disaster. His name is mentioned last in the list of apostles in Matthew 10, as well as in all of the other lists, along with a comment about his betrayal of Christ. The dark story of Judas is a blight on the page of human history. His name became a byword for betrayal, and has become so despised that it is not used in human society—although its meaning is full of loveliness.

I believe this man can teach us some profound and awakening lessons, so let's examine what the Bible says about him.

1. His name

   a) Judas

   The name Judas, a common name, was simply the Greek form of Judah—the land of God's people. Some say the name comes from a root meaning "Jehovah leads," while others think its root has reference to "one who is the object of praise." Either way, it's a paradox! If it means "Jehovah leads," there was never an individual who was more obviously led by Satan than Judas. If it means "one who is the object of praise," there was never an individual more unworthy of praise than he was.

   b) Iscariot

   The name Iscariot basically comes from a combination of the Hebrew term *ish*, which means "man," and Kerioth, the name of a town. He was "a man from the town of Kerioth." It's simply a geographical identification.

   It's interesting that Judas is the only apostle who is identified geographically. This is important because he is the only non-Galilean, the only Judean Jew. Since the rest of the apostles were from Galilee, it may indicate that from the very beginning Judas was never really one of the boys. Also, southern Jews from Judea usually felt themselves greatly superior to the rural Jews of Galilee, so Judas might have looked down on the other apostles with a pride that deepened as time went on.

Twenty-three miles south of Jerusalem and seven miles from Hebron was a small cluster of tiny farming villages. As these villages grew together they formed a little town called Kerioth—a town that would one day give birth to a child who would become the most hated human being who ever lived.

2. His call

The call of Judas is not recorded in the Bible. The first time he's mentioned in the gospels is right here in the list of Matthew 10. We don't even know how he got in the group. Now, we *do* know that the Lord called him, but we don't know any of the circumstances.

a) Judas's commitment

It's obvious that Judas was attracted to Jesus. He followed Him and stayed with Him longer than a lot of the other false disciples who bailed out much earlier. In fact, in John 6 there are many disciples who follow Jesus, but when He demands total commitment out of them, verse 66 says, "From that time many of his disciples went back, and walked no more with him." But the twelve remained. So, when Jesus called for an all-out commitment and many of the disciples left, Judas stuck it out—he stayed.

Judas was definitely attracted and committed to Jesus— but not on a spiritual level. I believe he was attracted on a selfish level because he saw what Jesus could do for him. Judas saw His power and believed that He would bring the kingdom. And of course he wasn't interested in the kingdom for the kingdom's sake or for Christ's sake, he was interested in the kingdom for what he might gain from it if he were on the inner circle. He followed and was committed, but he was totally motivated by selfish purposes.

b) Jesus' choice

From Judas's perspective, he chose to follow Jesus, but from Christ's perspective, Judas was chosen to follow. It's the same paradox of human choice and divine sovereignty that is present in salvation. We come to Christ because we choose to believe (John 6:37, 40), yet we are chosen before the foundation of the world by Him (Eph. 1:4-5). This is a paradox that is ultimately solved only in the mind of God.

One thing is certain—Jesus knew Judas would betray Him, and that's why He chose him. You see, Jesus knew the plan. Not only was He omniscient, but He knew the Old Testament had predicted that one of His own would betray Him.

(1) Psalm 41:9—"Yea, mine own familiar friend, in whom I trusted, who did eat of my bread, hath lifted up his heel against me." The psalmist saw the Messiah being betrayed by His own familiar friend, far in the future.

(2) Psalm 55:12-14, 20*b*-21—"For it was not an enemy that reproached me; then I could have borne it. Neither was it he that hated me that did magnify himself against me; then I would have hidden myself from him; but it was thou, a man mine equal, my guide, and my familiar friend. We took sweet counsel together, and walked unto the house of God in company. . . . he hath broken his covenant. The words of his mouth were smoother than butter, but war was in his heart; his words were softer than oil, yet were they drawn swords." Here we see treachery, hypocrisy, and betrayal, with a messianic perspective.

(3) Zechariah 11:12-13—"And I said unto them, If ye think good, give me my price; and if not, forbear. So they weighed for my price thirty pieces of silver. And the Lord said unto me, Cast it unto the potter—a lordly price that I was prized at of them. And I took the thirty pieces of silver, and cast them to the potter in the house of the Lord."

The Old Testament prophesies that the Messiah would be betrayed by His own familiar friend for thirty pieces of silver, and the New Testament simply records the fulfillment of prophecy (Matt. 26:14-16). So when Jesus chose Judas, He knew that he would be the one to fulfill the prophecies of betrayal. He chose him because of the plan.

In John 17:12, Jesus is praying to the Father about the twelve, and He says, "While I was with them in the world, I kept them in thy name; those that thou gavest me I have kept, and none of them is lost, but the son of perdition, that the scripture might be fulfilled." In other words, Judas was lost because it was the fulfilling of Scripture. Jesus chose him because He knew the Scripture, and He knew that prophecy must be fulfilled. That was the plan!

If the betrayal was prophesied, was Judas responsible?

You say, "How can God predetermine that Jesus would be betrayed, set up the plan, make all the prophecies, fit Judas into it, and then make him responsible?" I don't understand it because I don't have the infinite mind of God, but Judas *is* responsible. Look at Luke 22:21-22. Jesus, speaking at the Last Supper, says this: "But, behold, the hand of him that betrayeth me is with me on the table. And truly the Son of man goeth, as it was determined; but woe unto that man by whom he is betrayed." On the one hand it was all determined, but on the other hand Judas was responsible.

The overruling power and providence of God can allow such a man as Judas to desire to follow Christ of his own choice, and yet be in utter fulfillment of the divine plan. That is the power of God!

    c) Judas's character

Outwardly, I don't think Judas appeared to have a defective character. In fact, he must have had qualities and capacities that commended him. He was with the disciples for three years, and when Jesus announced (John 13) that one of them would betray Him, they didn't suspect Judas—they suspected themselves. They had no more reason to suspect Judas than they had reason to suspect themselves. Judas must have been a fantastic hypocrite. So good, in fact, that they elected him treasurer of the group. That just shows you how much they trusted him.

You say, "Well, they must not have known about the rotten, sinful background he must have had to do such a wretched and vile thing to Christ. He must have had a track record that was horrifying!" Well, he probably didn't start off any worse than some of the others. Matthew was an extortioner and a thief, and Simon the Zealot was possibly an assassin. The whole group was kind of a crummy bunch if you look at it that way.

Judas must have put on an act of hypocrisy to end all acts. It's interesting that he never had a word to say until he complained about the money that Mary wasted on anointing Jesus' feet (John 12:3-6). This is the first time he opens his mouth in the entire biblical record. He must have guarded his mouth well, in order not to give himself away.

Judas had the same potential as any of the others. Christ could have transformed him—if his heart had been willing. He had the same raw material and was no more unqualified than the rest. *But the same sun that melts the wax, hardens the clay.* While the other men were being melted and molded, he was being hardened!

He was probably a young, devout, zealous, patriotic Jew who didn't want the Romans to rule, and he saw in Christ an opportunity to follow one he believed was the Messiah. He thought Jesus would set up His earthly kingdom, overthrow Rome, and reestablish the days of prosperity and glory to Israel. Judas followed Jesus for the crass, materialistic possibility of getting in on the gravy train. He was never really drawn by the person of Christ, to believe in Him and to love Him; he only saw Him as a means to an end—gain for himself. All he saw was the road to personal prosperity.

d) Judas's chance

Jesus chose Judas because of the plan, yet He offered Judas every opportunity *not* to fulfill it. Judas heard the lessons that Jesus taught in the three years that he was with Him, and many of them directly applied to him: the lesson of the unjust steward (Luke 16:1-13); the lesson of the wedding garment (Matt. 22:11-14); and lessons about money (Matt. 6:19-34); greed (Luke 12:13-15; 12:16-21); and pride (Matt. 23:1-12). Jesus even said, "One of you is a devil" (John 6:70*b*), to warn Judas. But Judas never listened and never applied the lessons. He just kept up his deceit.

Jesus knew exactly what Judas was, yet He still loved him and tried to reach him. A perfect example of this is in John 13 during the Last Supper. In verse 21 Jesus says, "Verily, verily, I say unto you that one of you shall betray me." In verse 25, John asks Jesus who it is that will betray Him, and He answers in verse 26, "He it is to whom I shall give a sop, when I have dipped it." The sop was a piece of bread that was soaked in a jam-like paste made out of fruit and nuts. It was a common practice in the Orient for the host of a meal to give the honored guest the sop. So, when Jesus gave the sop to Judas, He was honoring him, respecting him, loving him, and lifting him up. I believe it was an act of love and affection. So, besides teaching and warning Judas throughout His ministry, Jesus actually honored the man. He was always reaching out to Judas—but he never responded!

3. His progress

The only definite allusions to Judas during the interval between his call and the events around the betrayal are recorded in the gospel of John. From there we can follow the progressive disaster of Judas.

a) The setting

(1) His desire

In the three years that Judas was with Jesus, he must have thought that the kingdom would come at any moment. He saw Jesus perform miracle after miracle after miracle—people were healed, the blind could see, the deaf could hear, the lame could walk, the dumb could talk, people were miraculously fed. Judas saw that Jesus obviously had the power to bring in the kingdom. And because he was so greedy, he tenaciously hung in there just waiting for it to happen.

I would hasten to add that he is no different than the other twelve in this respect. They all believed that the Messiah had come to bring an earthly kingdom and that He would overthrow Rome. They all believed that they had met the Lion of the tribe of Judah who would usher them into the glory of the kingdom. But the Lord had to tell them that before He fulfilled His role as the Lion, He had to fulfill His role as the Lamb slain from the foundation of the world. And as He talked about dying, giving His life, and being lifted up, I can just hear Judas saying, "What's He talking about?"

(2) His disillusionment

I believe the incident that finally destroyed Judas was what occurred after Jesus' triumphal entry into Jerusalem. When Jesus rode into the city the people "took branches of palm trees, and went forth to meet him, and cried, Hosanna! Blessed is the King of Israel, that cometh in the name of the Lord" (John 12:13). When Judas saw the people acknowledging Jesus as King he must have thought, "This is it! It's finally going to happen—today! Jesus is going to overthrow Rome and set up the kingdom. It's about time!" But instead of ushering in the kingdom, Jesus started referring to His death with the statement, "Verily, verily, I say unto you, Except a grain of wheat fall into the ground and die, it abideth alone; but if it die, it bringeth forth much fruit" (John 12:24). When Judas heard this, I believe he was literally devastated. This was the last straw! I think it finally became clear to him that it wasn't going to happen, so he sold his soul to hell.

b) The sequence

(1) His hatred unmasked

An incident that occurs in John 12 serves to unmask the hatred that had built up in Judas. We read in verse 3, "Then took Mary a pound of ointment of spikenard, very costly, and anointed the feet of Jesus, and wiped his feet with her hair; and the house was filled with the odor of the ointment."

In response to Mary's act, we see the first time Judas opens his mouth in Scripture: "Then saith one of his disciples, Judas Iscariot, Simon's son, who should betray him, Why was not this ointment sold for three hundred denarii, and given to the poor?" (vv. 4-5). By this time, Judas hated Jesus so deeply that he couldn't stand any homage paid to Him. What started as attraction, love, and fascination, became frustration and finally turned into hate. Why? Because Jesus didn't do what Judas had expected.

Then in verse 6, John makes an editorial comment, under the inspiration of the Holy Spirit, regarding the motive of Judas' complaint: "This he said, not that he cared for the poor, but because he was a thief, and had the bag, and bore what was put in it." Judas didn't become a thief at this point; he had always been one. He had probably been stealing money (the Greek literally says "pilfering") from Jesus and the apostles for the three years he had been with them.

Can you imagine the kind of person he was? He traveled around with this poor band of men, and while they were doing good, he was stealing out of their resources. He had absolutely no love or affection for them. He was a materialist, and he was in life only for what he could get out of it—and he got it any way he could.

That night, Judas left Bethany, initiated his first fatal interview with the chief priests, and negotiated to betray Jesus for thirty pieces of silver. It's interesting that in the same night, the Lord was anointed out of love and betrayed out of hate. And may I hasten to add that it is still so with every man. Christ is either enthroned or betrayed—there's no middle ground. Men either pour out their love to Him, or sell Him for whatever price they have deemed proper.

(2) His hypocrisy exposed

After having negotiated the betrayal, Judas joins the rest of the disciples in the upper room (John 13) and plays the role of the hypocrite to its fullest extent. In the first part of the chapter, Jesus washes the disciples' feet (including Judas's), and then begins to expose his intent: "Ye are clean, but not all of you. For he knew who should betray him; therefore said he, Ye are not all clean" (vv. 10b-11). Then in verses 18-19, Jesus continues to expose Judas: "I speak not of you all (I know whom I have chosen), but that the scripture may be fulfilled, He that eateth bread with me hath lifted up his heel against me. Now I tell you before it come, that, when it is come to pass, ye may believe that I am he." Jesus told His disciples what was going to happen, so that when it did, they would realize that only God could have known.

Even though Jesus was in the process of exposing Judas, the following account shows how effective he was in his hypocrisy: "When Jesus had thus said, he was troubled in spirit, and testified, and said, Verily, verily, I say unto you that one of you shall betray me. Then the disciples looked one on another, doubting of whom he spoke. Now there was leaning on Jesus' bosom one of his disciples, whom Jesus loved. Simon Peter, therefore, beckoned to him, that he should ask who it should be of whom he spoke. He, then, lying on Jesus' breast, saith unto him, Lord, who is it? Jesus answered, He it is to whom I give a sop, when I have dipped it. And when he had dipped the sop, he gave it to Judas Iscariot, the son of Simon" (vv. 21-26).

John is usually the one referred to as the one "leaning on Jesus' bosom," and I believe that John is the only one who heard Jesus' statement about the sop. I don't think any of the others heard it, because if they had, they probably would have attacked Judas when he was given the sop. Instead, verses 27-28 tell us, "And after the sop Satan entered into him. Then said Jesus unto him, What thou doest, do quickly. Now no man at the table knew for what intent he spoke this unto him." Nobody knew why Jesus sent him away. According to verse 29, "some of them thought, because Judas had the bag, that Jesus had said unto him, Buy those things that we have need of for the feast; or, that he should give something to the poor." He played out his hypocrisy so well, that they still didn't suspect him as the betrayer.

Well, Satan entered Judas, and Judas went out to consummate the betrayal.

4. His betrayal

    a) Established

        (1) A private place

Judas didn't act in a moment of passion or insanity. His dark deed was quietly and deliberately planned. Matthew 26:16 tells us that after he bargained with the chief priests, "from that time he sought opportunity to betray him." Mark 14:11 adds, "And he sought how he might conveniently betray him." And then in Luke 22:6 we read, "And he promised, and sought opportunity to betray him unto them in the absence of the multitude."

Judas was afraid of the crowd. He saw all the people flock to Jesus during His triumphal entry into Jerusalem, and he was afraid of what they might do to him. So he planned to betray Jesus in a private, out-of-the-way place.

        (2) A pitiful price

According to Matthew 26:15, Judas negotiated with the chief priests for thirty pieces of silver—exactly what Zechariah 11:12-13 had prophesied. Thirty pieces of silver would be worth somewhere between ten and twenty dollars today. The small sum that Jesus was betrayed for tells me three things: (1) greedy people will settle for any price; (2) the chief priests had such disdain for Judas that they wouldn't give him a larger sum; and (3) they hated Jesus so much that that's all they thought He was worth.

(3) A personal perversion

Judas negotiated that he would point Jesus out to the chief priests in a secret, quiet place, in the pitch dark of night. And the sign he gave them was: "Whomsoever I shall kiss, that same is he" (Matt. 26:48).

b) Executed

The next time we see Judas is in John 18. Jesus was in the garden of Gethsemane with His disciples when Judas entered the picture. In verses 2-4 we read, "And Judas also, who betrayed him, knew the place; for Jesus often resorted there with his disciples. Judas then, having received a band of men and officers from the chief priests and Pharisees, cometh there with lanterns and torches and weapons. Jesus, therefore, knowing all things that should come upon him, went forth, and said unto them, Whom seek ye?"

Jesus knew that Judas was going to betray Him with a kiss. So, He just removed the necessity for the kiss by walking out and saying, "Whom seek ye?" But just to show you the pit of blackness in the heart of Judas, Matthew 26:49 tells us that Judas kissed Him anyway!

Why did Judas sell Jesus? Well, he had malice, worldly ambition, revenge, hatred of what was good, rejection of what was pure, pride, ingratitude, and anger—but mostly, he had greed—crass, worldly materialism.

5. His death

Judas sold Christ, he sold his fellow apostles, he sold his own soul, and he bought hell. Unfortunately, the price was too high. Matthew 27:3 says, "Then Judas, who had betrayed him, when he saw that he was condemned, repented, and brought again the thirty pieces of silver to the chief priests and elders." The word "repented" might sound good to you, but the Greek tells us that he just "felt bad"—he regretted what he had done. Now, a spiritually-minded man deals with his conscience in a spiritual way and goes to God for forgiveness. But a crass materialist like Judas deals with his conscience in a physical way. So instead of going to God and asking forgiveness, he returned the money, thinking that the physical act of returning the money would relieve his spiritual conviction. But it didn't! His unforgiving heart screamed out for vengeance on himself. Verse 5 tells us, "And he cast down the pieces of silver in the temple, and departed, and went and hanged himself."

Acts 1:18 says of Judas's death, "And falling headlong, he burst asunder in the midst, and all his bowels gushed out." Some people think this is a contradiction. It's not! Judas couldn't hang himself any better than he could do anything else. Either the knot was insufficient or the branch broke. Having hanged himself over a precipice, he plummeted to the rocks beneath, bursting open his bowels.

By the way, do you know what the chief priests did with the money Judas returned? According to Matthew 27:6-7, "the chief priests took the silver pieces, and said, It is not lawful to put them into the treasury, because it is the price of blood. And they took counsel, and bought with them the potter's field, to bury strangers in." That's an exact fulfillment of Zechariah 11:12-13. The plan was fulfilled.

6. The lessons learned

   a) Judas is the world's greatest example of lost opportunity

   Twelve men had the privilege of walking for three years in the presence of the living God incarnate. Eleven of them took the opportunity to turn to Him, but Judas missed it. There are people today who live in the presence of Christians—and thus live in the presence of Christ—who eventually lose the opportunity to turn to Christ and go into eternity without Him. Judas was the worst, but those who continue to pass up opportunities are just following his example. He stood in the fairest surroundings the world has ever known, and he was content to associate—nothing more. And because of that, he's damned forever!

   b) Judas is the world's greatest example of wasted privilege

   Judas wanted money, riches, and possessions. He could have possessed the universe forever, but he sold it for ten or twenty dollars. God offers all men the riches of eternity. Have you said no to His offer and yes to some pittance that will burn in the end along with this earth?

   c) Judas is the world's greatest illustration of the love of money being the root of evil

   He loved money so much that he actually sold the living God. That's how far greed can take a man. Judas is a monument to the destructiveness and damnation of greed.

d) Judas is the world's greatest lesson of the forbearing, patient love of God

Only God could have known what He knew, and tolerated that man's presence for as long as He did, and still reached out to him in affection and offered him the sop—and even called him "friend" after his kiss of betrayal. Judas gives us incredible insight into the patience forbearance of God.

e) Judas provided an essential qualification in preparing Christ for His role as our High Priest

Hebrews 2:17-18 says, "Wherefore, in all things it behooved him to be made like his brethren, that he might be a merciful and faithful high priest in things pertaining to God, to make reconciliation for the sins of the people. For in that he himself hath suffered being tempted, he is able to help them that are tempted." Many men are betrayed and wounded in the house of their friends. When they go to the Lord and say, "Lord, do You understand what has happened?" He can honestly sympathize. Part of the perfecting of His high priestly work came in having to endure what He endured from Judas.

Judas was the ultimate hypocrite of all time—an illustration of people who can hide in the presence of Christ and be filled with Satan. Acts 1:25 says that Judas went "to his own place"—right where he belonged. And it's the same place all men who reject Christ end up.

Focusing on the Facts

1. What does the name Judas mean? Why is it a paradox that the man who betrayed Jesus was called Judas (see p. 99)?
2. What does the name Iscariot mean? Why is it important that we know Judas's surname was Iscariot (see p. 99-100)?
3. Many disciples had followed Jesus, but what happened to them when He demanded their total commitment (John 6:66; see p. 100)?
4. Why was Judas attracted and committed to Jesus (see p. 100)?
5. Why did Jesus choose Judas to follow Him (see p. 101)?
6. What did the Old Testament prophesy about the betrayal of Christ? Support your answer (see p. 101).
7. How was Judas responsible for his actions when the betrayal was predetermined by God (Luke 22:21-22; see p. 102)?
8. Why didn't the other disciples suspect Judas when Jesus said that one of them would betray him (see p. 102)?

9. Could Christ have transformed Judas? Why did Judas never become transformed (see p. 103)?
10. When Jesus offered the sop to Judas in John 13:26, what was He doing to Judas? Why (see pp. 103-4)?
11. In what way was Judas no different than the other disciples (see p. 104)?
12. What statement by Christ devastated Judas's belief that Christ would usher in an earthly kingdom (see p. 105)?
13. Why did Judas's fascination for Jesus finally turn to hate? How did that hatred manifest itself (John 12:3-5; see pp. 105-6)?
14. According to John 12:6, what kind of man was Judas? How long had he been that (see p. 105)?
15. How did Jesus expose the hypocrisy of Judas (John 13:10-11, 18-29; see p. 106)?
16. How did Judas plan to betray Jesus (Luke 22:6; see p. 107)?
17. What three things does the amount of the betrayal money indicate (see pp. 107-8)?
18. What was the sign of Judas's betrayal (Matt. 26:48; see p. 108)?
19. Why did Judas sell Jesus (see p. 108)?
20. Matthew 27:3 says that Judas "repented." What does that mean (see pp. 108-9)?
21. What did Judas eventually do to relieve himself of his guilt (Matt. 27:5; see p. 109)?
22. What lessons can be learned from Judas's life? Explain each one (see pp. 109-10).

Pondering the Principles

1. Judas was a hypocrite. He was such a good hypocrite that none of the disciples suspected him of being one. Do you play the game of hypocrisy? List as many situations as you can think of in which you are presently being hypocritical. In each situation, isolate your motives. What should your motives be? List those situations in which you are not hypocritical. Isolate your motives in each of those. What are the significant differences between being hypocritical and being genuine? Make the correct motivational changes in your walk with God.
2. Jesus did everything He possibly could to reach out and show His love to Judas, even though He knew Judas would betray Him. How do you treat those who may not treat you right? Do you still show your love to them, or do you respond negatively to them? What would Christ want you to do? If there are some people you are presently not giving honor to, then begin today to seek for ways to honor them. Be faithful to follow the Lord's example with Judas.
3. According to Matthew 27:3, Judas repented, but not in the way that we think of it. He felt sorry for what he had done, but he didn't go to

God to ask forgiveness. What do you do when you have sinned? Do you just feel sorry for what you have done, or do you honestly confess your sin before God and desire to turn from it? Read 2 Corinthians 7:8-10. According to the apostle Paul, what is the difference between godly sorrow and the sorrow of the world? If there is any sin in your life that you have not truly repented of, confess that now and turn from it completely.

4. Review the lessons that can be learned from Judas's life (see pp. 109-10). Which lessons can be applied to your life? In what ways? Begin to apply those lessons today. Thank God that you can be a better follower of Christ from seeing the errors of Judas's life.